ON HAVING
THE TIME
OF YOUR LIFE

On Having the Time of Your Life

J. Wesley Brown

LUMINARE PRESS
WWW.LUMINAREPRESS.COM

On Having the Time of Your Life
Copyright © 2024 by J. Wesley Brown

All rights reserved. This book or any portion thereof may not be reproduced or used in any manner whatsoever without the express written permission of the publisher, except for the use of brief quotations in a book review.

Printed in the United States of America

Luminare Press
442 Charnelton St.
Eugene, OR 97401
www.luminarepress.com

Additional sources:

E. E. Cummings, *A Selection of Poems*.
New York: Harcourt, Brace & World, 1961.

D. H. Lawrence, *Selected Poems*.
New York: Viking Press, 1959.

Louise Erdrich, *The Painted Drum*.
New York: Harper, 2006.

Oxford Annotated Bible.
Oxford, UK: Oxford University Press, 1962

LCCN: 2024913190
ISBN: 979-8-88679-634-6

This book is dedicated to the students, colleagues, and friends who through the years have asked me questions, thereby inviting me into the time of their life. By doing so, you became significant participants in the time of my own life. This also includes Jenny and then Kathiann who, sequentially, shared eighteen and then forty-four years of my married life. This includes my three children, now each into their seventh decade of life, who continue to enrich this time of my life with their love, their care, their laughter, their children, and their grandchildren. I am grateful to all of you for allowing the time of my life to begin and to end each day with this prayer, "Thank you, God, for another day of loving."

Contents

Preface and Biographical Note | ix

ADVENT
Prescription for a Holiday Season | 3
Virgin Births and Christmas Spirits | 9

CHRISTMAS
What Child Is This? | 17

EPIPHANY
Epiphany! Getting It! | 25

LENT
A Koan for Christians | 35
Forgiveness: The Bridge We Must Cross | 41
Perfection! Really? | 49
Remembering Jesus | 55
Soul Food | 61
It's Not Easy Being Green | 67
Natural Righteousness | 73
A Faithful Ecology | 81

EASTER
Easter. Again. | 89
"Christ of the Commonplace" | 95

PENTECOST

    Being the Church | 105

    A Telling Witness | 109

ORDINARY TIME

    On Having the Time of Your Life | 117

    Religion 101: G-O-D | 123

    Good News for Parents | 129

    A Geography of Love | 135

    A Sermon for Earth Day | 141

    Reflections on Psalm 23 | 149

    The Personal God | 153

A COLLEGE OF THE CHURCH

    Homily for the Opening of the Academic Year 1995-96 | 159

    Members One of Another | 163

    Getting to Know Me | 169

    Hearing Voices | 177

    Know Thyself | 183

    Royalties Statement | 189

Preface and Biographical Note

The sermons in this book were each preached to a particular congregation at a particular time and place sometime during the past sixty years. I hoped that each sermon would be relevant to the experience of those particular people there and then. In choosing to reprint the sermons here I hope that readers will find something relevant to their own lives and experience as I reflect upon the meaning of the biblical texts. I recommend you read the biblical text before reading the sermon based upon it.

The sermons preached to a church congregation are grouped according to the seasons of the liturgical year. The settings were United Methodist and United Church of Christ congregations in California, Hawaii, and Minnesota, where I was appointed to work. When I retired in 1996, we moved to Santa Barbara, California, and I served one year as an interim associate minister for the First United Church of Christ there. In 2013 we moved to the Rose Villa Retirement Community and joined the Kairos United Church of Christ in Milwaukie, Oregon, where I was invited, at times, to preach and lead worship.

Sermons that were preached at the Saint Olaf College Chapel services, held five mornings a week during the academic year, reflect the experiences of students and faculty in their life and work together in that fine college of the church.

My own preparation for ministry began in Methodist parsonages in North Dakota where my father, C. Maxwell Brown, and my mother, Dorothy Brown, provided a home of secure love, encouragement, and inspiration for Christian living for my two sisters, my older brother, and me. My father's self-discipline included spending one hour in his study for every minute in the pulpit, a practice that enabled him to extend his ministry through radio broadcasts in North Dakota and in Northern California in the 1960s.

My academic experience included graduation from Fargo Central High School, 1954; College of the Pacific, BA, 1958; Drew Theological Seminary, Master of Divinity, 1961; and a PhD from the Graduate Theological Union in Berkeley, California, in 1972.

ADVENT

Prescription for a Holiday Season

Isaiah 12:2–6; Philippians 4:4–7

There is a difference between good news and good advice. It is good news when your doctor tells you that you have the blood pressure of a marathon runner. It is good advice when he tells you to lose forty pounds. It is good news when your child tells you she has straight As at school for the fourth year in a row. It is good advice when your financial adviser tells you to start saving one hundred dollars per month now for your fourth-grader's college education.

We don't always receive good advice as joyfully as we receive good news. We receive good news with joy and gratitude and contentment. We receive good advice with the sense that we had better make some decisions and change the way we have been acting.

Today's reading from the lectionary is one of those passages of scripture that delivers good advice based on the good news of Emmanuel, that God is with us. I regard this passage from Paul's letter to the Philippians as a prescription for the holidays, good advice from Dr. Paul of Tarsus to be followed by anyone who might want to receive the gift God seeks to give us at Christmas. And as with any prescription from a doctor, you need to read the directions and follow the directions carefully if you hope to receive the benefit. So, this morning I want to think with you carefully about Dr. Paul's prescription for the holidays. Let's look at what he says.

"Rejoice in the Lord always." Paul says it twice! "Again, I will say, rejoice!" It is as if he can hear the thoughts of those who receive his letter. "Yeah, right. Get serious, Paul. You have been shipwrecked three times, beaten with rods three times, received thirty-nine lashes five times, imprisoned more times than you can remember, exiled, stoned, on trial for your life, betrayed by friends and enemies alike. *You* are telling us to rejoice? Always rejoice in the Lord?"

I know, it hardly seems reasonable that Paul could say such a thing. But that is what Paul says, "Rejoice in the Lord, always." You heard me right, rejoice. And he can say it precisely because of the trials he has endured. He is no Pollyanna insisting that life is always wonderful when, in fact, life is often hard. Do you remember the story of Pollyanna—the glad girl—who found something to be glad about in everything that happened to her? I could never stand those stories about Pollyanna when I was a kid. She was too good to be true!

She was like the little girl whose parents were trying to cure her annoying optimism. So, for her Christmas present, the parents filled their garage full of horse manure and on Christmas morning said to her, "Your present is in the garage, go find it." The little girl came back from the garage bubbling with joy. "Oh Mommy, Daddy, with all that manure in the garage I just know there has got to be a pony in there somewhere!"

Paul is no Pollyanna. He has known suffering and betrayal in life. But he is credible, he is believable, he can tell us to rejoice because he has experienced also the gift of Emmanuel, that God is with us no matter what the circumstances of our life may be.

The second part of Dr. Paul's prescription for the holidays is this, "Let your gentleness be known to everyone." "Let your gentleness be known to everyone." That is interesting!

Have you ever asked yourself what you would like to be known for? Your beauty? Let your beauty be known to everyone? Your wit? Let your wit be known to everyone? Your intelligence? Your talent? Your wealth? Your power? Your garden? Your match-box collection? What? What would you like to be known for?

Paul's prescription is, "Let your gentleness be known to everyone." Holidays are times when we may become known for our pushiness, for our determination to get things done, for our ability to do everything we always do plus twenty additional things. I don't ever remember seeing an increase in gentleness on the freeways or in the shopping malls during the holidays. Quite the contrary. What I see more often is an increase in competitiveness, in greediness, in assertions of power in trying to have one's own way, or to outdo someone else in giving the best gifts.

Gentleness is an interesting quality to contemplate. Gentleness expresses a deep sense of security, of confidence, of poise, as well as sensitivity to others around you. Gentleness is not weakness. It is, rather, the strength of self-control not to force our own will, or our own way. Gentleness is expressed in the confidence that we do not need to force our way, in the confidence that there is a greater power at work than either you or the persons around you possess.

As Paul puts it, let your gentleness be known to everyone—the Lord is near. There is a confidence and a security that gives rise to gentleness in the knowledge that Emmanuel, the Lord, is near, that God is with us in every situation of life.

Part three of Dr. Paul's prescription for the holidays is this: "Do not worry about anything, but in everything by prayer and supplication with thanksgiving let your requests be made known to God."

If you stood in the mall holding a sign that said "Let Nordstrom solve your holiday worries," no one would think it peculiar at this time of year. They would think it just another form of advertising. Both your holding the sign and the message on the sign would be quite in context for these next two weeks. Right?

But if you stood in the mall with a sign that says, "Do not worry about anything," you would be laughed at as the kookiest of the kooks in kookooville. "What do you mean, 'Don't worry about anything'?! Do you know how many people I have yet to shop for? Do you know how many people are coming to spend Christmas with me? Do you know I haven't even decided what to cook for

Christmas dinner? It's Christmas! I'm going nuts here! What do you mean 'Don't worry about anything'?"

I don't know who said it first, but it is true. Worry is a misuse of the imagination. Paul would agree. Paul said, "Do not worry about anything." Instead, do something else with your imagination. Instead of using your imagination to worry about all the "what ifs" that rarely happen, "by prayer and supplication with thanksgiving let your requests be made known to God."

Well, here we are with Dr. Paul's prescription. You don't benefit from the prescription by setting it down with all the notes by your telephone and forgetting about it. You do what the prescription tells you to do. "By prayer and supplication with thanksgiving let your requests be made known to God."

If you want the cure for galloping holiday worries you will follow Paul's prescription.

I don't believe that prayer is me telling God what God needs to learn about me and what I want. I believe that prayer is opening myself to God so that I can learn what God already knows about me and my wants. I find that when I pray there is usually a great sorting out of things in my life, that what I want gets sorted out from what I need. And when I get clear about the difference between what I need as opposed to what I want, I am not anxious anymore. God provides what I need.

Dr. Paul is just passing on what Jesus taught his disciples. Do not be anxious about what you will eat, or what you will drink, or what you will wear, your heavenly Father knows all these things. Which of you by being anxious can add a day to your life, or one inch to your height? Seek first God's kingdom and all its gifts will be yours as well.

Don't worry. Rather, pray, directing your mind into the clarifying and healing presence of God. Rejoice always, for God is near.

This is the prescription that will turn any holiday, indeed, turn any day into a Holy Day. And what does Dr. Paul tell us will be the result if we follow the prescription?

"And the peace of God, which surpasses all understanding, will guard your hearts and your minds in Christ Jesus."

The gift of the peace of God from the Prince of Peace. This is what we may expect for Christmas this year if we follow Paul's prescription for the holidays.

This is what Phillips Brooks wrote about in his beloved Christmas carol:

> No ear may hear his coming,
> But in this world of sin
> Where meek souls will receive him—still,
> The dear Christ enters in.
>
> Oh Holy Child of Bethlehem
> Descend to us we pray
> Cast out our sin and enter in,
> Be born in us today.
>
> We hear the Christmas angels
> The great glad tidings tell,
> O come to us,
> Abide with us,
> Our Lord, Emmanuel.

Virgin Births and Christmas Spirits

John 3:1–8; I John 4:7–13

My wife and I had the wonderful experience of visiting some of the great museums in our country: The Metropolitan Museum of Art in NYC, the Boston Museum of Fine Art, the Norton Simon and Huntington museums in Pasadena. In those museums we saw religious images from Africa, Central America, and Asia as well as Europe.

These were pictures and carvings and sculptures and masks that had, at some point in their history, the power of religious symbols, images that drew their observer into the experience of mystery and power. That is what religious symbols do. They enable the worshipper to participate in the spiritual power of that religion. That is what makes them religious symbols and not merely a sign or a poster or a pretty picture. Religious symbols, like music, engage us at a level deeper than words can convey.

But symbols can lose their power as gateways to religious experience. They can devolve into mere signs of a season, or sentimental background to what is of ultimate importance, what is holy in a culture. They can become a kind of sensory clutter that assaults our eyes and our ears for a few weeks a year.

This morning I would like us to think together about religious symbols, how they have the power to engender religious experience in us, but also how they can lose their power as symbols, how they cease to be places where the experience of God breaks into daily life.

It is clear to me that the symbols of Christmas have lost the power to connect and to transport many people to a transcendent, sacred space. Stories of angels singing in the sky, of a star that moves slowly and stops over a particular stable in a particular Middle Eastern village; a virgin betrothed to an old man gives birth to a child, a child who flees into Egypt with his family, but returns from Egypt, like Moses of old, to save his people. These were symbolic stories of such power and significance that the early church incorporated them into its sacred texts.

These are stories that, on the face of them, ought well to stun us into awed silence and wonder. But for many among us, the stories of Christmas leave us merely stunned, exhausted, wondering not at the divine mystery in life but wondering whether all the fuss is worth all the effort. Indeed, I think it is what contemporary folk consider to be miraculous in the Christmas stories that has caused them to lose their power as religious symbols. "Virgin birth? Get serious! Biologically impossible! If I must choose between the science of biology and believing in virgins conceiving children, forget it. I'm not going there!"

In talk like this we see that a powerful symbol of the first-century world has lost its symbolic power and has been reduced to a literal description about human biology and, thus, wisely dismissed as biologically impossible.

But when we do this, we are ignoring what the symbols meant to the people who first used them in their own culture. For those people a virgin birth was one way of accounting for and pointing to a reality they had experienced, an experience that was too deep for mere descriptive language.

And yet, I think what virgin birth signified can still be meaningful to us today, indeed, what it has meant in Christian experience can once again kindle that rebirth of wonder that is at the heart of Christmas, that is at the depth of all religious experience. So, what did the symbol of a virgin birth mean two thousand years ago? And what, if anything, might it yet mean for us?

Let's start by looking at what the stories meant in the context where they were first told, the early centuries at the beginning of our Common Era. For starters, we need to know that not all the Gospel writers use the virgin birth as a symbol. Each Gospel writer was addressing a different audience and was answering different questions about who Jesus was and about the meaning of Jesus's life.

Mark's Gospel has no story at all of Jesus's birth. Mark's Gospel begins with Jesus being baptized by John in the Jordan River, and the spirit of God descending on Jesus like a dove, and a voice from heaven saying to him, "Jesus, you are my beloved son. I am well pleased with you." No virgin birth. No angels. No stars. Instead, it all begins with a baptism and an experience of the spirit of God, an experience, says Mark's Gospel, that is available to all who would become followers of Jesus.

John's Gospel has no birth stories either. Rather, John's Gospel begins with a poem of praise in which the eternal, creative wisdom of God takes human form and dwells on earth, a source of grace and truth for all humankind.

Matthew's Gospel begins with a genealogy tracing Mary's lineage back to King David, and with Joseph having a dream in which he hears that the young girl he is betrothed to is pregnant. But the angel in his dream tells him not to reject her, not to divorce her, because the child she carries will be the savior of the nation Israel, a child who fulfills an ancient prophecy of a savior of the nation, a child who is, himself, the sign that God is with them. It is only in Matthew's stories that wise men come to honor a new king of the Jews. In Mathew's Gospel the holy family flees to Egypt to escape King Herod's killing the baby boys in Bethlehem. Jesus teaches his followers at a gathering called The Sermon on the Mount, not Mount Sinai, like Moses delivering the Ten Commandments, but on a hillside in Galilee, with the eight beatitudes and teachings that fulfill the spirit of the Mosaic Law. All these stories in Matthew are cited as examples of ancient Hebrew prophecies being fulfilled, to validate the authority of

Jesus as the new Moses, the new deliverer, the new teacher, the new lawgiver for the Jewish people.

It is in Luke's Gospel that we find the elaborate stories of an old woman conceiving a child, and of a young virgin conceiving a miraculous child, and of that child's birth being announced by angels singing in the heavens, a birth attested to by simple shepherds and by a wise old man and by a prophetess living in the temple of Jerusalem. This is the child who, at age twelve, amazes the elders of the temple with his wisdom, and who, at age thirty when he is baptized by John, experiences the spirit of God descending upon him in the form of a dove. These stories are told to validate the authority of Jesus as a divine hero, on a par with and superior to the Greek gods and heroes of the Roman Empire.

In the centuries immediately before and after Jesus's birth, to be born of a virgin was not about biology, nor about sexual abstinence, nor exceptional sexual virtue. The great warrior Alexander the Great was said to have been born of a virgin. Augustus Caesar, ruler of the Mediterranean world, was proclaimed in word and in stone to be divine, a son of god, the savior of the world. In those times in those cultures to be born of a virgin was the Good Housekeeping Seal of Approval, the Underwriters' Guarantee, the lifetime warranty, the Oscar/Golden Globe, Heisman Trophy for superhero divinities — you were the *Son of God*. To tell the story of the significance of Jesus in the Greco-Roman world required that Jesus be no less than the son of a god, born of a virgin. That was how the story had to be told to symbolize the truth, the ultimate meaning of Jesus's life and teaching in the experience of those who followed him.

So, note this, the virgin birth story is not the most common nor consistent symbol in the Gospels to express the origin of Jesus's power and authority. The most common and consistent symbol in the Gospels is the story of the Holy Spirit of God indwelling Jesus at his baptism. The consistent story of Jesus and of the preaching of the early church is that the spirit of God made manifest in the life and teachings of Jesus transforms human lives, makes life anew, like being born again, a virgin birth not of the flesh but of the Spirit.

The Gospel of John repeats this truth again and again. In the story of Nicodemus that I read this morning, John is quite specific about this. When Jesus tells Nicodemus that he must experience a rebirth from heaven, Nicodemus asks him point-blank: "Can a man enter again into his mother's womb and be born again?" And Jesus answers with great patience: "No. What is born of the flesh is flesh, what is born of the spirit is spirit." I'm not talking about physical rebirth. I am not talking about a fleshly virgin birth. I am talking about a transformation of life brought about by the Spirit of God indwelling your life. "The Spirit blows where it wills, and we hear the sound of it but we do not know from whence it comes nor where it goes. Thus it is with everyone who is born of the Spirit."

The miraculous birth is the birth of love, the gift of God's Holy Spirit in the human heart. As we heard read this morning from the first letter of John, "Where love is, God is, for God is love." Those who know love know God, for God is love. Love is not one thing and God another. If you experience love, you experience God, and as you express love you are an agent of God's love.

The French theologian Gabriel Marcel said: "Every experience of love is an experience of God. Every experience of truth is an experience of God." This miraculous birth—this virgin birth, if you will, is the continuing gift of the spirit of God in human life, the experience of love in our lives, making life new, raising us from relationships of despair, incorporating us in communities of love, families of love, the community of Emanuel, of God with us, the community of the church.

We have been singing about this meaning of a virgin birth all Advent season:

> "Oh holy child of Bethlehem, descend to us we pray,
> Cast out our sin and enter in, be born in us today.

Virgin Births and Christmas Spirits

We hear the Christmas angels the great glad tidings tell.
O come to us, abide with us, our God, Emmanuel!
How silently, how silently the wondrous gift is given.
So God imparts to human hearts the blessing of his heaven,
No ear may hear his coming, but in this world of sin,
Where meek hearts will receive him still, the dear
    Christ enters in.

"Hark, the herald angels sing 'Glory to the newborn King.'
Peace on earth and mercy, mild,
God and sinners reconciled.
Born to raise all folk on earth.
Born to give us second birth."

Put another way, the virgin birth is an internal event in the hearts of women and men. It is the experience of accepting reconciling love. As such, it is deliverance from the messianic expectation that God will come and save us someday but, rather, getting it—really getting it—that God has already entered our history, and that the love we experience moment to moment and day to day is the presence of God with us. It is that experience that saves us, and it is that experience—that love—that is the hope of the world.

Our experience of love is not the whole of God, any more than our taste of the ocean is the whole ocean. But it is a taste, it is participation in the reality of God. The experience of love is an experience of the truth that God is with us. That is what the virgin birth means to me today, in the closing days of the year 2010.

Have you experienced a virgin birth this Christmas? Have you experienced the gift of love? Have you witnessed it? Have you known a truth in your life that is deeper than words, that is more precious than any gift found at the mall, that you would not return or exchange for anything?

Think about it.

CHRISTMAS

What Child Is This?

John 1:1–14

When my daughter Laurie was almost two years old, we gave her a rubber dolly that had arms and legs that moved and hair that was a bright orange color, the strangest color hair I had ever seen on a doll, the color you might expect in an electric carrot.

Laurie didn't seem to mind. She loved the doll, and she named her dolly "Violet Mary." She bathed Violet Mary, and she dressed Violet Mary, and she even took her little blunt scissors and gave Violet Mary a haircut that made her look like a punk rocker dolly thirty years before there was punk rock music. Still, Laurie loved Violet Mary with all the passion of her little two-year-old heart.

I was serving a church in a little town in Northern California at that time, and when Christmas drew near, we put together a Nativity scene, using the Mary and Joseph figures we had, and using the children's stuffed animals for the animals in the stable. We didn't have a baby Jesus doll of the right size, and so, in my hopeful naivete, I swaddled Laurie's doll in a receiving blanket and put it in the manger, thinking Laurie might be pleased that her doll had been given the starring role in the Nativity scene.

When Laurie saw the crèche, she studied it for a few moments and then declared indignantly: "That is not the baby Jesus. That is Violet Mary!"

What I learned from this was that when it comes to telling the Christmas story you need to make the story appropriate to your audience. Some people will accept no substitute for the child in the manger story. For them, the innocent vulnerability of the newborn child is central to the mystery of Christmas. For other people, the child in the manger is a lovely tale but is in no way necessary to the Christian faith. It is even OK if it is Violet Mary.

Does this surprise you? I would suggest this morning that it should not surprise us, because two of the four Gospels of the New Testament make no mention of the birth of Jesus at all, and the two Gospels that do tell of Jesus's birth tell quite different stories about it.

Mark's Gospel makes no mention of the child Jesus at all. Mark begins with Jesus already a grown man, coming to the Jordan River to be baptized by John the Baptist, then calling his twelve disciples, then starting to preach, to cast out demons, and to heal the sick and the lame.

Jesus announces God's reign by the signs and wonders he performs, and by his amazing powers evokes the confession of faith from the disciple Peter, "You are the Christ. You are the Messiah." Were we to rely only on Mark's Gospel for an answer to the question, "What child is this?" Mark would answer, "What child are you asking about?"

Matthew's Gospel begins with a genealogy tracing Jesus's lineage from Abraham, the original Jewish patriarch, to King David and ultimately to Joseph, the husband of Mary. This genealogy is divided into three parts, each part being fourteen generations long. When this number fourteen is multiplied by these three parts, the total is the same number as the numeric value assigned to the three letters in King David's name written in Hebrew. Wow! Do you think that is just a coincidence?

According to Matthew's Gospel, Jesus fulfills the prophecies of the coming Messiah found in the Hebrew Bible. Further, in Matthew alone, Joseph has a dream that warns him to take Mary and the baby Jesus into Egypt to escape being murdered at the hands of the pharaoh—oops, I mean King Herod. So, it is only in Matthew's

Gospel that Jesus comes out of Egypt, takes up residence in the promised land, and delivers his teaching in five major sermons—just like the five books of Moses—the Torah. In Matthew, Jesus is referred to as a rabbi, a Jewish religious teacher.

What child is this? For Matthew, Jesus is the Messiah descended from King David, the fulfillment of prophecy, the new Moses, greater than Moses. Matthew tells a story that will impress Jewish believers living in and around Jerusalem. It is a Gospel designed to bring Jewish believers into the new Christian community.

Luke has quite a different audience in mind for his Gospel. Luke traces Jesus's lineage back to Adam, not Abraham; all humankind is involved here, not just the Jews. A heavenly being, the angel Gabriel, tells Mary that she will bear a child, and heavenly choirs herald Jesus's birth in Bethlehem. Luke was, himself, a Gentile convert to Christianity who traveled with the apostle Paul. Luke's Gospel shows Jesus reaching out to Samaritans, to women, to Romans, to the gentile world. Luke makes fewer references to Hebrew prophecies being fulfilled because this would not be important to the Gentiles to whom Luke was writing. This is probably why Jesus is not called "rabbi" in Luke's Gospel, but rather, he is called "master."

What child is this? For Luke he is the miraculously born hero, come to announce the reign of God to all people—all people, not just men, and not just the Jews. He dies on the cross not with words of despair, "My god why have you forsaken me!" but with dignity and purpose, "Into your hand I commit my spirit."

What child is this? This child is the Son of God, more than equal to any of the Greek and Roman gods of that era. In Luke's Gospel he is a universal savior.

And then there is John's Gospel, the prologue to which I read this morning. There is no birth story in John's Gospel. There is, rather, an introductory poem about what the Greeks called "the Logos," which is translated as "the word" in our English Bible.

But this translation is not up to the job. The Logos for the Greek world at that time was the divine, rational, organizing principle of the whole creation. This Logos, John says, was made flesh and came to dwell among us.

It would be like someone today saying: "The DNA of the whole biological order, and the atomic structure of all being, and the secret of gravity and whatever energies there are that hold the cosmos in order have been revealed to us. That which makes the cosmos rational and makes human reason possible lives among us in Jesus. The Logos—the eternal mind of God—has been expressed to the world in a way the world can understand it, full of grace and truth. The light of the eternal mind of God shines forth from this man into the darkness of creation, and the darkness has never overcome it. The light shines on!" The verb tense in the Greek text expresses the continuous present. God's light continues to shine on in the darkness!

This is why Jesus says in John's Gospel: "I am the light of the world. Those who follow me will never walk in darkness." Jesus says: "I am the living water. Those who drink of me will never thirst." Jesus says: "I am the bread of life. Those who partake of me will never hunger." Jesus says: "I am the way, the truth, and the life. Those who know me know the Father who sent me, for the Father and I are one."

What child is this? To the second-century audience, familiar with Greek philosophy and Greek mystery religions, John's answer is, Jesus is the eternal mind of God, made known and made knowable, to you and to me!

Wow! What a story! But there is no birth story in John's Gospel.

So, the four Gospels tell different stories about how Jesus of Nazareth came to be called Jesus the Christ. That's so. But, so what? Why am I telling you this on Christmas Day, 2005?

For two reasons, really. The first is to remind us that these stories were not scripture from the moment they were written. These stories became Christian scripture because they spoke to different people, of different cultures, with different understandings of God. These stories became Christian Gospels because each one pointed to what people experienced when they followed the way of Jesus. They found their way to healing. They found their way out of madness. They found a teacher who opened to them a way to understand their lives in relation to the great mystery of God. They found their way into a community that included them, that accepted them whatever their race, whatever their nationality, whatever their gender, or their family, or their personal history. They learned of a love so great that not even death could overcome it. They found a way of living that was like being born again.

What child is this? The human imagination stretched to its limits to find words to express who this child is: the Messiah, the Christ, the Risen Savior, the Son of God, the Eternal Word made flesh. What words would you use to answer the question?

Which brings me to the second reason I have told you about the four Gospels this morning. I have done so to remind you that people from the very beginning have needed to use the tools they had, the language, the stories, the ideas of their own cultures to express what was true for them about Jesus and the mysterious power he called "Abba, "dear father," whom in English we call God.

What child is this? We, like members of every generation before us, answer this question using the words, the images, the songs, the rituals that have come before us, and, inevitably, the very lives we live in our own time and place. How do we answer the question, What child is this?

Some people sing it. Hear the music.

Some people paint it. See the pictures. See the banners.

Some people dance it. Watch the children.

Some people preach it. (My favorite teacher said: "Faith is an acoustic affair. It occurs by hearing the word.")

Some people teach it. Marcus Borg says, "Jesus is the human face of God."

Some decide to act out their answer in legislatures where the needs of the poor, the disabled, the abandoned, the disenfranchised are remembered, protected, and provided for. Remember those women and those men.

Christmas is filled with sentiment. But Christmas is never, never sentimental, because the Word is born into the darkness of this suffering world, and the light that enlightens all humankind shines on, shines on in the darkness of the world. The light shines in the darkness, but the darkness does not overcome it.

What child is this? This is a question whose answer is as large and as small as the lives with which we live our own answers.

I like Howard Thurman's answer:

"When the song of the angels is stilled,
When the star in the sky is gone,
When the kings and princes are home,
When the shepherds are back with their flock,
The work of Christmas begins.
To find the lost,
To heal the broken,
To feed the hungry,
To release the prisoner,
To rebuild the nations,
To bring peace among the brothers and sisters,
To make music in the heart."

May the light of God shine on, shine on, shine on in our hearts made bright by love of the Christmas child.

Christmas, 2005

EPIPHANY

Epiphany! Getting It!

Isaiah 60:1-6; John 1:1–18

This is Epiphany Sunday, that Sunday in the church year when Christians celebrate the recognition that the child born in the manger of Bethlehem is the Messiah. It is about the epiphany of Jesus as the Christ in our own life that I want us to think about for a few moments this morning.

Epiphany. The word means a revelation, a disclosure, truth from the depth arising to the surface, a whole new perception of the way life is. Every epiphany, by its very nature, casts into the shadows some older way of perceiving life, some former self-understanding, some former way of living our life in the world. This is why epiphanies are often painful, exposing as inadequate or as an illusion some notion we had formerly clung to as the truth about life. Furthermore, epiphanies don't occur in public space. Epiphanies are not the kind of thing that can be recorded by a video camera. Epiphanies are events that take place in our internal space, in our internal history.

Now, the whole New Testament is about the early church's attempt to articulate the meaning of the Epiphany of Jesus, that recognition in a person's internal history that Jesus is the Messiah, or the Christ, which is how the word "Messiah" is translated into Greek. The Gospels say that when the epiphany takes place it is like the blind seeing, the deaf hearing, the lame walking. It is like being born again. It is an event of the spirit, an internal event, wherein the old way of being is cast aside and one sees and hears and walks in a radically new way.

But there are two passages in the Gospels that are particularly associated with the Epiphany, the revelation of Jesus as the Christ. One passage is the first chapter of John's Gospel, which I have just read. The other is the story of the visit of the three wise men, as told in the second chapter of Matthew's Gospel, about which Linda has sung this morning.

You could hardly find two more different texts. First, there is Matthew's spare story of three sages of the ancient world, astrologers, who are told by Herod, the Jewish puppet king of the Roman Empire, to go to the village of Bethlehem, great King David's village, where, the Hebrew prophets had said the Messiah, the new deliverer of Israel, would be born. The wise men come to Bethlehem, but they find no young prince in a palace. They find a young peasant in a stable.

But for them, it is an epiphany! *This* child, in *this* place is the promised Messiah! They present their gifts, and, disobeying the king of the realm, Herod, they sneak out of the country to find their way home. They have been changed by their epiphany. And no sooner do they leave the scene than Joseph has a dream in which an angel tells him to flee away to Egypt and to take Mary and the baby into Egypt with him.

Why is it that only Matthew, within the whole New Testament, tells this story of the three kings? The answer lies in a repeated refrain we also find again and again in Matthew's Gospel: "This was done to fulfill what the Lord said through the prophet, 'Out of Egypt I called my son.'" The epiphany, the revelation, so far as Matthew is concerned, is that Jesus is the Jews' Messiah, the one who fulfills Jewish prophecies, the one who is a descendant of the great Jewish king, David, the one who like the nation's founder, Moses, comes out of Egypt to save his people and who, as a new Moses, is the great teacher of the law. Only, says Matthew, Jesus is greater than Moses. He not only fulfills the prophecies, but he extends the meaning of the Mosaic laws. "You have heard it said of old, but I say unto you" is how Jesus teaches in Matthew's Gospel. Even the structure of Matthew's Gospel falls into five parts, like the five scrolls of the law given by Moses. By its content and by its structure, Matthew's Gospel proclaims the epiphany of Jesus as the Jewish Messiah, the new Moses, the new David, the revealer of a new covenant with Jews who, as followers of Jesus, become the new Israel, the new people of God.

This is epiphany. This is revelation. This introduces a whole new self-understanding of a people into history. The old way of living is past. Jews, stop looking to the future for the One to come who will change your life. The child in the manger is not the Messiah you expected. But he is the Messiah who has been given! The new way of living is here, now! God's reign is now! When you get that, there is an epiphany in your life. The old has passed away, behold, the new has come.

Matthew's Gospel is about the epiphany, the revelation of who Jesus is to the faithful Jews of the first century. It was how Matthew tried to help his Jewish companions "get it."

While this might make sense as a strategy to explain Jesus to Jews who looked for a Messiah to come, it would make very little sense to gentiles, who shared none of the history of the Exodus, nor of Moses, nor of King David.

The good news of Jesus was not preached only to Jewish believers. The good news of Jesus was preached in a multicultural, multireligious world, a world very much like ours today in that it was a world of competing visions and philosophies and interpretations of life. One of the powerful religious philosophies of the first century was called Stoicism. It preceded the Christian Gospel by more than two hundred years and had a multitude of adherents throughout the Mediterranean world. When John wrote his Gospel, he was writing not so much to people whose self-understanding had been Jewish, as he was writing to gentiles, whose self-understanding was Greek, and Stoic in particular.

The people to whom John was writing were bright, inquisitive people, just as you are. They wanted to know what life is about, just as we do. They wanted to know why the world works as it does, just as we do. They wanted some principle by which to live that would enable them to really live their life, just as we do.

People in this Greek culture believed that their minds shared something in common with all things in the created world, a common principle they shared with all things, a part of the structure of all things, giving order to all things. Because it was within their own minds as well, it made all things intelligible. The Greeks called this creative, organizing power that gave form and structure to all things the Logos. If you understood the Logos, you understood the eternal, fundamental, organizing, rational principle of all things in the whole created world.

That marvelous prologue to John's Gospel, which I read this morning, is really a summary of the common sense of the Greek community of that day. In the beginning was the Logos. It was not only with God, it was God. All things were created through the Logos, without the Logos nothing was made that was made.

"Well, yes," said the Greeks. "Of course. We know. Tell us something new!"

And John does! He writes that the Logos, the divine ordering, creating principle of God, the eternal wisdom of God, became flesh and dwelt among us, and we have beheld his glory. The true light that enlightens every man and woman has come into the world. To know who Jesus is, that Jesus is the Logos in the flesh, is to know God. To know Jesus is to know God, for Jesus is the eternal Logos of God-made flesh. Epiphany! The divine principle of the whole created order is revealed, and that divine, ordering principle—the Logos—is love!

John's Gospel is not about angels and shepherds and Jewish kings and the fulfillment of Jewish history. John's Gospel is about the eternal wisdom of God disclosed to the whole world, told in a way that would communicate the Christian Gospel to the

Mediterranean world steeped in Greek cultural self-understanding.

"In the beginning was the word, and the word became flesh and dwelt among us. That word is the light of all humankind, a light that shines on in the darkness and which the darkness has never overcome. 'I am the light.' 'I am the bread of life.' 'I am the water of life.' 'I am the way, the truth, and the life.' 'If you know me, you know the Father who sent me.'" These are the words we find only in John's Gospel, for in John's Gospel it is the eternal creative love of God that walks among us. As it was in the beginning, is now, and ever shall be. Amen!

Epiphany! You sophisticated gentiles who hunger for the bread of life, do you get it?

But what about us, who are neither Jew nor Greek? What about us, Americans in a multicultural, secular society, standing at the eve of the twenty-first century? Can there be an epiphany for us? How does the child of Bethlehem become the Christ for us, become the first and final word about the way life is—for us?

Well, it seems to me that human beings today still long for that event that will put an end to longing, that will fulfill the earnest desires of their human hearts. That human longing for that sense of completion, fulfillment, abundance in life. That longing, which took the form of hope for a Messiah in ancient Israel, is alive among us in 1999. It seems to me that the desire for some epiphany, some revelation that will make clear the point of it all, the desire for some word to be spoken, some bread to be offered, some light to be cast upon the shadowy, ambiguous pathway of our lives is as widespread in 1999 as it was in the first century.

That longing for some future, delivering event takes many forms in our culture: When I get out of school, when I finally can leave home, that is when life will really begin. When I get a real job, with a real paycheck, that is when life will be good. When I'm finally married, that is when…no; when we have a child of our own, that is when life will really begin. When the children finally leave home, when they are off to college and out of the house, that is when life will begin. When we burn the mortgage. When I get that promotion and we can buy that little place in the mountains we have always wanted, that is when life will be glorious. When I retire, then, finally, at last, life will be what I have always imagined it would be. When my ship comes in—and each ship for which we long is still over the horizon, and life, real life, abundant life, is not yet here. We await its coming, eagerly, longingly wait. That is the messianic hope at the end of our century.

And the Logos? Surely some scientific breakthrough, some revelation of the human genome, some yet unimagined feat of genetic engineering will make intelligible all mysteries, all possible meanings. Surely, I can't live *this* life abundantly. Why, I'm bald! I have fat thighs! My neck is too long! My memory is too short! Politicians are creeps! Surely some Logos, some *word* will make clear our place in the universe, correct every imperfection. Sometime. Sometime later. It hasn't happened yet. What we have here is uncertainty, what we have here is ambiguity. What we have here is life amidst struggle, and imperfection, ignorance, and suffering and death.

But for some, there is an epiphany. "I will be no closer to life next year than I am in this instant. That mysterious Power that 'ises' all things is 'ising' me, now!" Eternal life does not begin in some sweet by and by. Eternal life is in the precious, unrepeatable, here and now that God is giving me. The Christ is not found in some posh palace in some distant time and place. The Christ is in this straw-strewn manger, here, now. In this congregation. In this family. God does not promise us some super life tomorrow. God gives us this life, today. The epiphany of Jesus as the Christ happens within our internal history. Epiphany happens when we "get it." Jesus is Emanuel, God is with you. God is with me. Emanuel. God with us. Now.

As it was in the beginning, is now, and ever shall be!

A few years ago our pastor invited members of this congregation to receive the gifts we are given in this life, to really receive them, so that we might really live those gifts, day to day, in this world.

That Sunday she had each member of the congregation select a paper star from the offering plate on which was printed one of the gifts that we have been given. I invite us all to do this again this morning. I invite us to do it to move beyond the messianic longing for a life we do not have into an appropriation of the meaning of life we do have. I invite you to focus on this one word, this specific gift this year, to meditate upon it, and then to incarnate that word in your own life, to consciously embody God's gift in your own flesh and blood, and thereby to change history.

John wrote: "The Light shines on in the darkness, and the darkness has never overcome it." Never overcome it! Not in the first century. Not in the tenth century. Not in the twentieth century.

Let the light of God's gifts to you shine on in the world. Let this word of God's love be your special calling this New Year. Let there be an epiphany, a disclosure of Emmanuel to the world, wherever you walk.

Amen.

LENT

A Koan for Christians

Matthew 5:43–48, I Corinthians 13

"Show me the face you had before your mother and father were born." This is what Zen Buddhists call a "koan," a statement or question that is used to disable one's usual, rational approach to understanding reality. The idea is that when we give up our habitual way of thinking about the world, we are then ready to perceive the world as it really is. Serious meditation on a koan, so the Zen practitioner would tell us, is a path that leads to understanding the world in a new way.

This morning I invite you to think with me about a kind of Christian koan, a statement that may help us understand more truly what it means to be a follower of Jesus. The koan is this: "Show me the faith of a Christian before there was Christian faith." In the last few decades, Christian scholars have been working on this koan-like problem.

You see, what you and I have come to accept as the Christian faith is a body of teaching and beliefs and practices that developed over a period of several hundred years after Jesus's life on earth.

The early followers of Jesus weren't called "Those people who believe the Bible is the infallible, literally true word of God." No! They couldn't have been, because there were no agreed-upon Christian scriptures until the middle of the second century.

Early followers of Jesus were not called "those people who believe what the creeds of the church say." They couldn't have been. The creeds were not written until two hundred years after the New Testament scriptures had been assembled and agreed upon.

"Show me the faith of a Christian before there was Christian faith." To be able to do this we need to try to understand what society was like at the time those first followers of Jesus lived. We need to understand what those early followers of Jesus did that made them such a powerful movement in that society. What did they do that attracted so many adherents that by the end of the first century the Romans arrested and killed them for being a threat to the empire? What was so radical and attractive about them that by the early fourth century, Christian faith was declared to be the official religion of the Roman Empire? What was the faith of Christians before there was Christian faith?

This question has been pursued in depth by a New Testament scholar named John Dominic Crossan. He talked about this question in his Earl Lectures in Berkeley in 1995 and published his remarks in 1998 in a book titled *The Birth of Christianity: Discovering What Happened in the Years Immediately after the Execution of Jesus.* I will share a few things from this interesting book that I think are pertinent to this season of Lent and which are relevant on this "One Great Hour of Sharing" Sunday.

Let us begin by noting that in both secular and scriptural texts from the first century, the early Christians were called "Followers of the Way." That they believed certain things is undoubtedly true, but it was their way of living, the things that they did, how they behaved that attracted notice.

Followers of the Way were people who practiced certain ways of living; they differed from the people around them in the ways they related to other people. It was a way of living that flowed from Jesus's teachings gathered in the fifth chapter of Matthew's Gospel, and that culminate in that portion I read as a text this morning. "Be perfect, therefore, even as your heavenly Father is perfect." It is clear from the context that the kind of perfection Jesus is talking about is perfection in love, to be perfect in love.

The apostle Paul introduces this way of living by saying "Let me now show you a more excellent way." For Paul, perfect love means showing patience, kindness, and humility, not insisting on having your own way, not being arrogant, rude, resentful, not taking pleasure in what is wrong or false but rejoicing in what is true. To live this way might be too much to expect of children, Paul says, but we are not children. We are adults who, knowing as we do that we do not see and understand everything clearly, should not behave as if we did! Paul closes this chapter on love by saying, "Pursue love—and strive for the spiritual gifts."

Professor Crossan points out that the first-century Followers of the Way showed this radical love in the ways they related to one another and to the society around them. In particular, they showed this love in the ways in which they ate.

Followers of Jesus ate with everyone. By observing the simple but essential act of eating we can learn a great deal about life in any society. Who is it that eats? How often do they eat? How much do they eat, and with whom do they eat?

I have never been unwillingly hungry in my life. There have been a few times in my life when I have chosen not to eat, but that was a fast I could break whenever I chose to do so. It is not that there was no food available to me if I wanted it.

That is a very different circumstance than that faced by millions of people in Jesus's day, just as it is in our day when twenty-five thousand people a day die on this planet from hunger and malnutrition. Millions of people in the colonies of Rome did not eat every day, not because they would not have liked to but because they could not afford to. The Romans sent shiploads of grain, oil, and wine out of Palestine back to Rome and other urban centers of their empire, but the poor of Palestine knew hunger as a daily reality. In Jesus's day—then as now—access to food can stand as a sign of access to power. If you have power you control resources, you can decide how to distribute your resources, you can invest, you can save, you can barter, you can buy food. By the same token, if you do not have power, if you do not have resources, if you do not have something to spend or barter you are very likely not to have food.

Sharing the food they had, eating together, breaking bread together, and passing the cup were acts of love that distinguished Followers of the Way. The Gospel stories of Jesus feeding the hungry crowds, feeding the disciples on the Sabbath, eating a final Passover meal with his disciples were recorded by the earliest church because they were events in which the inequalities of power and status were set aside in order to meet the basic needs of hungry, poor people. It is very instructive to read the Gospels with this in mind, and to note the variety of ways in which Jesus contradicted the social order by his actions and his teachings about food.

What we share at our communion table, in a ritualized, symbolic way, points to the basic need for sustenance that was recognized and acted upon by Followers of the Way. It was one of the things that distinguished Christians before there was Christian faith.

There is a second thing having to do with food that distinguished early Followers of the Way. It is this.

Followers of Jesus ate with everyone. The radical behavior that was a hallmark of Jesus's ministry—his inclusion of women, of Samaritans, of fishermen, of Roman bureaucrats—was continued by Followers of the Way when they gathered to eat. Everyone was welcome to eat in the new community. The act of everyone eating together was itself an embodiment of that new social order Jesus called the Kingdom of God. It was a challenge and a threat to the social order and hierarchy of the time.

Think about it. Whom do we sit down to eat with every day? When we eat, we tend to sit down with members of our own race, our own economic class, our own educational level. Do we sit down for lunch with the janitors and window washers at our offices? It never happened at the colleges where I taught. There is a sorting out of social classes at the restaurants we frequent, is there not? Are the people you sit down with at Denny's the same people you sit down with at El Encanto? I don't think so.

Certainly, there are economic differences at work here, but economic differences, as we know, are markers for educational differences, which are markers for racial differences, which are markers for a myriad of social differences, from prison populations to corporate board members. The point is, who we eat with says much about how permeable and flexible the boundaries of our social identity are, who we trust as family, who we willingly admit to the intimate table where food is shared.

When Followers of the Way sat down to eat with Jew and Greek, slave and free, male and female, children and aged, the social elite and the off-scourings of society, they constituted a new social reality—a new way of being in Roman society that was characterized by ethnic, economic, tribal, and religious differences. Jesus's counsel to be perfect in love was made real in the lives of the people who shared those meals in those moments. "Be perfect, even as your Father in heaven is perfect!" This teaching, which appears to be about individual piety, is about social transformation.

Before I could be ordained as a Methodist minister, I had to answer a question directly related to this text from Matthew. The question was this; "Do you expect to be made perfect in love in this life?"

Did *I* expect to be made perfect in love in this life? Did I expect to be made *perfect* in love *in this life*? Some question!

This question, which every prospective Methodist minister must answer, is itself a kind of koan for Christians. To answer "Yes" sounds, on the face of it, terribly arrogant and presumptuous. "Why, yes. I expect to be made perfect in love in this life."

But to answer "No" is to say you don't believe God is able to change your life, which is to say you think you are more powerful than the love of God, which is no less arrogant and presumptuous.

There have been hundreds of sermons exploring this problem preached in Methodist churches for the last three hundred years. I am not going to preach another one this morning.

But my point is this. The Followers of the Way seem to have taken the question seriously and, in doing so, enabled God's love to work among them, to transform them, and eventually to transform Roman society. The man for whom I am named, John Wesley, believed Followers of the Way could and should answer this question *"Yes,"* and those who followed his lead helped to transform eighteenth-century English society. John Wesley gave this advice to the Followers of the Way who were called Methodists: "Do all the good you can, to everyone you can, in every way you can, for as long as you can."

I do not know how deciding to live as a Follower of the Way might change your life—might change our life. But I do know, without a doubt, that to live daily with the expectation that you can be made perfect in love will change your life and will change the world around you.

As we gather around this table this morning to break the bread and to share the cup in One Great Hour of Sharing, let us eat and drink together as Followers of the Way.

Amen.

Forgiveness:
The Bridge We Must Cross

Luke 7:36-50

The Gospel text for this morning is titled "A Sinful Woman Forgiven." Another Bible in my office calls the story "Jesus Anointed by a Sinful Woman." These little titles are not, of course, parts of the biblical text itself but are inserted by editors and publishers of these editions of the Bible in the hope they will help us, the readers, know what the text is about. But if anything is clear in Jesus's teaching, there are no "sinful women," except where there are sinful men; and the woman in this case is mentioned only at the beginning and the end of the story. Further, she has no lines, she speaks no words. The story, it seems to me, is not just about a sinful woman, but about three people: a woman, a Pharisee whose name is Simon, and Jesus. Let me read the text. Luke 7:36-50

This story of Simon the Pharisee's dinner party for Jesus describes another of those dramatic encounters that distill centuries of Jewish teaching about the love of God into a single event. It is not, however, a story of interest to everybody. If you are a person who has never done something you should not have done, this story is not for you. Or, if you are a person who has never left undone something you should have done, this story will only bore you. Or, if you have never felt that glow of self-righteous satisfaction when someone you know is found to be slightly morally compromised, you may want to take a nap now. (We'll wake you in time for the offering.)

But if you are someone who knows the pain or the shame of having done those things you ought not to have done, and have left undone those things you ought to have done, or, if you feel you have been wronged by another person and are not entirely unhappy enjoying what you believe to be your moral advantage over this person, then this story may well be of interest to you. Since I am a person convicted on all three counts, it is a story of great interest to me.

Here is the situation. Jesus has been invited to dinner by a Pharisee named Simon. Now, right away, there is something odd about this picture—not that Jesus has been invited to eat, but that it is a Pharisee who has invited him to his home. Pharisees, we recall, were those good, religious folks who strove, in all sincerity, to lead pure lives, to be punctilious in observing all the refinements of the Jewish law. Usually, we meet Pharisees as Jesus's adversaries in debate. Here we see Simon the Pharisee as Jesus's host at a dinner party. What is going on here?

The text says that Jesus was reclining at the dinner table, lying down, head toward the food, feet toward the edge of the room, as was the custom when enjoying a feast in this outpost of Roman culture, the city of Capernaum. A woman slips into the room and, standing at his feet, begins to weep. Why? She is so taken up in her emotion that her tears flow, wetting Jesus's feet as he reclines at the table. She stoops. She dries his feet with her hair. She kisses his feet. She pours perfumed ointment on his feet!

How did she get in here? Why didn't the servants stop her? Is she as familiar in this house as she is in the streets of Capernaum? Simon recognizes her, but instead of speaking to her, asking her to leave, he mutters to himself, "Clearly this Jesus is no prophet or he'd know the kind of woman that is touching him—that *she* is a sinner." Is this whole dinner party a setup to test Jesus? Perhaps this is why Simon had invited Jesus, not out of hospitality, but to assess just who this wonder worker is. In any case, Simon has lowered his opinion of Jesus, "He is no prophet!"

Jesus says nothing to the woman, either. Instead, he asks Simon a question: If two men owed money to a money lender, one a single month's wages and the other fifty months' wages, and the money lender said to them both, 'That's all right—forget it. You owe me nothing,' who would be more grateful? Who would love him more?"

That's a "no-brainer," for someone who audits life's accounts as carefully as Simon does. "The one who has been forgiven more, he's the one who will love the more."

"You are correct," says Jesus.

Then he turns to face the woman, but he speaks to Simon. "You invited me to your house for dinner, but you have not shown even the common courtesies one extends to a stranger, much less to a guest in your home. You provided no water to wash my feet. You provided no kiss as a sign of welcome; you provided no oil as a sign of honor. Every courtesy a host would offer, you have refused me. All that love and honor could offer, this woman has not ceased to give me since she walked in. Therefore, I tell you Simon, her sins have been forgiven; hence she loved much. But he who has been forgiven little, loves little."

Then, finally, Jesus speaks to the woman: "Your sins are forgiven"; (shocked muttering around the table); then, "Your faith has saved you; go in peace."

Let's look at each of the characters in this story. First of all, there is Simon the Pharisee. The Pharisees in their religious setting were much like mainline Christians in our own day. They weren't like the radical Zealots, plotting to overthrow the Roman government by force. They weren't the hyper-conservative Sadducees, committed to maintaining the old sacrificial system in Jerusalem's temple. They were observers of the Jewish moral laws and purity codes. With one eye on the laws and one eye on the world, they audited the moral character of everyone around them. Moral purity was the sign of a right relationship with God.

Now, good moral character is not a bad thing. But there are two problems with making it the focus of your religion. First, it tends to make you the center of your religious concern. Religion becomes all about me. How am I doing? Am I measuring up? Am I good enough? Am I pure enough? And second, it so quickly slides into the game of moral one-upmanship, of seeking and exploiting one's presumed moral advantage. (I may not be perfect, but I am sure better than she is!)

So, it is not surprising that the only words we hear from Simon are precisely this kind of moral auditing. Simon presumes he enjoys the moral advantage over this woman, this "sinner," as he called her. And he is quick to seize his presumed moral advantage over Jesus, "Surely he must know who this is that is touching him."

Simon's game is that if Jesus does not know who she is, Jesus is not as morally discerning as he himself is. Score one point for Simon!

And if Jesus does know who this woman is and lets her go on washing and anointing his feet, well, Jesus must not really care about being morally correct and upright. Another point for Simon! He sees himself as having the moral advantage: Score: Simon, two, Jesus, zero. This game could well end with Simon distancing himself from Jesus and from this woman, this "sinner," and thinking he has won!

But Jesus isn't playing the Pharisees' game. Jesus doesn't play the "who is the purest soul" game. Jesus doesn't play the "who is most righteous person in the room" game. Jesus is very clear that in the game of life no one enjoys a moral advantage in the eyes of God. Jesus was clear that no one wins the purity game. Ever! To drive the point home, Jesus said: "Men, if you look at a woman with lust, you've already committed adultery in your heart. Folks, if you are angry in your heart at another and call them a fool, you've lost. You're liable to the hell of fire."

Jesus made it very clear that no one can ever win at the purity game, and that no one may presume the right of moral advantage over others.

That is a hard game to let go of. There is that within me that is not entirely displeased at the moral lapse of my neighbors. There is that pharisaic voice in me that likes to pray, "O God I thank you that I am not like other men." There is that brother of the prodigal son in me who says: "Look Father, I've been the good guy. This other son of yours is the stinker. I'm the one who deserves the party."

But the Kingdom of God that Jesus announced is not entered by showing off merit badges. It is not a community of great purity. It is a community of great love. That's what Simon did not understand. It is what the woman in the story dared to believe.

What do we know about this woman? The text introduces her as "a woman who had lived a sinful life in that town." Simon recognizes her and classifies her as a general type, "the kind of woman she is—a sinner." We are not told how she merited her reputation; it's left up to us to project our worst imaginings upon her, and we easily slip into the Pharisees' disdain, "Oh God, I thank you I am not like this woman—this sinner."

What must life have been like for her, to have the first thing anyone thinks about you be that kind of a judgment? Can you imagine what it would be like to be so reduced as a person every day? So humiliated, day after day? To live a life so hemmed in by the judgments others make about you that they never come to know you.

How did she find the courage to enter Simon's house? Was it an act of desperation? Was it grief over a life from which she could find no way out, no way out in this cosmopolitan city where men paid for her body at night, and shunned her as a person by day, because it was she who was judged the sinner?

Jesus speaks first of all to Simon. "You have the logic correct in my little story about the two debtors. The one who is forgiven the larger debt *will* be the more grateful. But your head is disconnected from your heart, Simon. *Do you see this woman*? Not an abstract member of a class you call 'a sinner,' but *this* woman, flesh, tears, hair, hands? Look at the outpouring of her love. Does this not tell you how deeply she knows the forgiveness of God? She has loved much. Where does that love come from Simon? It comes from the God who has forgiven her much. Whoever is forgiven but little, loves but little." Simon, the game of life is not about purity, it is about love!

And Jesus says to the woman: "Your faith has saved you. Go in peace."

Let us look now at the third character in this story, Jesus. Jesus's teaching about forgiveness of sin is one of the things that most offended the religious people of his day. For Jesus, forgiveness of sin is never something negotiated in private with a cosmic, distant God. Forgiveness of sin is about life with our spouse, with our children, with our neighbors, with our brothers and sisters in the faith.

Consider these things Jesus said, "If you are at the altar about to offer your gift and you remember your brother or sister has anything against you, leave your gift at the altar, go, be reconciled to your brother or sister before you come before God with your gift" (Mt 5:22-23). Jesus said, "If when you pray you hold anything against anyone, forgive him so that your Father in heaven may forgive you your sins" (Mk 11:25). The prayer Jesus taught his disciples puts it plainly before us: "Forgive us our debts, as we also have forgiven our debtors." And the verses that follow read, "For if you forgive others their trespasses, your heavenly Father will also forgive you; but if you do not forgive others, neither will your Father forgive your trespasses." (Mt 6:12-15).

In these teachings Jesus aligns himself squarely in the tradition of the great prophets of Israel who stated again and again that it was not by religious observances and ritual purifications that people aligned their lives with the purposes of God. Rather, it was maintaining the bonds of the human community, welcoming the stranger, caring for the poor, lifting the weak, doing justice by the powerless, loving the neighbor that fulfilled the intent of the divine law.

Sin is forgiven, or not, in our relations with one another, and if we think we can be at peace with God and are not at peace with our neighbor, we are like whitewashed tombs, impressive on the outside but on the inside full of the stink of death itself. This was the predicament of Simon in our story this morning, more concerned with his own purity than in finding common ground with Jesus or with the weeping woman.

Our relationship is made right with God as we make right our relationships with one another. We are judged as we judge. The measure we give is the measure we will receive. We are forgiven as we forgive.

It is possible to be as pure as Simon the Pharisee, and just as loveless. But it is also possible to be exemplars of God's great love, as was the woman in this story.

The reconciling love of God is like a great stream that must flow through our lives to others if it is to cleanse our own lives.

Or, as the nineteenth-century English poet George Meredith put it, "He who does not forgive, breaks the bridge over which he himself must cross."

What does this mean for you?

What does this mean for me?

What does this mean for this congregation of faith?

God knows. And each one of us knows.

Let us, in prayer, acknowledge what we know.

Perfection! Really?

Matthew 5:43–48

September 26, 2018

"You, therefore, must be perfect, even as your heavenly Father is perfect."

This direction from Jesus to his followers comes right in the middle of what is called "The Sermon on the Mount." We might think that someone who first heard him say this thought: "You've got to be kidding! I have to be perfect as God the Father is perfect? He can't be serious!" And he got up, left the crowd, and went back down the mountain shaking his head.

But there it is, right in the middle of Jesus's teaching. "You, therefore, must be perfect, even as your heavenly Father is perfect."

Every Methodist minister, when he or she is ordained to the ministry, is asked these three questions by the ordaining bishop: 1. Are you going on to perfection? 2. Do you expect to be made perfect in love in this life? 3. Are you earnestly striving after it? Every clergyperson ordained in the Methodist Church is expected to answer "yes" to these three questions.

John Wesley expected every Methodist, not just the clergy, but every follower of Jesus to answer "yes" to these questions. Are there any Methodists here this evening? How is it going?

I am the son and the grandson of Methodist clergymen, so it is no mere coincidence that I was given the name John Wesley when I was baptized. John Wesley was the man who founded what came to be called the Methodist movement in Oxford, England, during the eighteenth century. I have been grateful that my parents decided to call me Wesley rather than John, since the name John Brown is popularly associated with a song about a body lying moldering in a grave, and there were enough problems growing up as a preacher's kid without having to deal with that song as well. But there is something about those three questions asked by that first John Wesley that is worth thinking about, and that is what I invite you to think about with me this evening.

First of all, the context in which Jesus instructed his followers to be perfect is his observation that God's love—God's grace—is extended to all people. Do not hate your enemy, Jesus says. Pray for them. Do not return evil for evil, but overcome evil with good. God is generous to the bad as well as to the good, making the sun to shine and the rains to fall on the just and on the unjust.

Do not be loving only to those who share your beliefs and your culture, Jesus told his followers. Even the gentiles do that. If you are to be the sons and daughters of your heavenly Father—which means to have the traits and character of your heavenly Father—you must love as God loves, "be perfect as your heavenly Father is perfect." Jesus's instruction is not about never making mistakes, we all make mistakes, not about always being right, none of us is always right. But be perfect in love, forgive others even as we are forgiven, so that we may be the sons and daughters of our heavenly Father.

Then there is the second question, that if you answer "yes" to the first question sounds like the height of arrogance and pride. "Do you expect to be made perfect in love in this life?" The usual shock of hearing this question comes at the end, hearing the words "in this life." Not eventually perfect in heaven, or miraculously perfect on our deathbed, but "perfect in this life."

But note, the question does not ask if I expect to make myself perfect. It asks if I expect to be made perfect, which is very different. It acknowledges that I cannot be a self-made man, that you will not be a self-made woman, but that another agent, some other maker, some other loving, creating, giver of life and maker of souls can make us perfect in love. The arrogance is not in the expectation to be perfect. It would be arrogant to expect that the God who created the heavens and earth and all that is in them could *not* perfect his love in a human life—that we are more powerful in opposition than is God whose intention and power is to create love. That would be the real arrogance.

Which leaves us with the third question, "Are you earnestly striving after it?"

Another way to put the question would be, If you expect to be made perfect in love in this life, do you sincerely want it to happen? Do you really want to be made perfect in love in this life?

You see, John Wesley was confident in the power of God to change a person's life, but he knew that people are quite capable of getting distracted by other concerns, quite devoted to other causes, quite capable of giving the time of their lives to acquiring riches, or power, or fame. Jesus himself faced this temptation at the outset of his ministry, you remember.

The tempter took Jesus to a high mountain and showed him all the kingdoms of the world in a moment of time and said all this could be his, if Jesus would worship him.

But Jesus said: "Be gone, Satan! It is written you shall worship the Lord your God and him only shall you serve" (Mt 4:10).

God can make one perfect in love in this life, but only if we want it to happen, only if we give the worship of our lives to loving what God loves. Or as the prophet Micah put it, by doing justice, by loving kindness, by walking humbly with God (Micah 6:8).

Is there something more worthy to strive for in life than to become perfect in love? Is there really something the people and creatures of the earth need more than to be humbly treated with justice and loving kindness? Is there really anything better to seek with our lives than to be made perfect in love?

It helps to be a member of a community that seeks to be made perfect in love, that strives to do justice, that acts with loving kindness, that humbly offers the time of its life to the service of what God loves, and that forgives one another even as it is forgiven when it falls short of perfection. I found this to be true growing up in a Methodist parsonage, as I am sure you have found it to be true in the faithful congregations you have been a part of throughout the years.

The authorities of the established church in England were not thrilled with John Wesley's devoted quest to be made perfect in love in this life. So, John Wesley went outside the doors of the established church to where the people were, to minister to them there. He preached outdoors at the entrances to coal mines. He organized classes to teach poor, illiterate people to read. He wrote pamphlets giving instructions on medical care for these poor people. He organized small groups of people to study and pray and look after one another. He didn't bring these people into the church. He brought the ministry of the church to where the people were, preaching the good news of Jesus's ministry of healing and inclusive love to the working poor of England.

The bad rap that accused Methodists of being fanatic pietists because they emphasized every Christian going on to perfection in love missed the truth that love is always a social phenomenon. There is always someone who is in need of love. It is the people whom God loves who change and change others as they strive to be perfected in love.

And how great that social change can be! Historians have said that it was the ministry of John Wesley in the eighteenth century that changed English society in ways that kept England from experiencing the kind of bloody revolution the French had in the nineteenth century. And in our society today we are being torn apart by people's worship of power, and fame, and wealth, and race who insist that they are right and their neighbors are wrong, that only people born in this country deserve to live in this country, and who proudly shout "God bless America." Indeed, God bless us all, that we may be made perfect in love.

For the common people who were called Methodists, John Wesley summarized the way to be made perfect in love in this life, in this way:

> "Do all the good you can,
> By all the means you can,
> In all the ways you can,
> In all the places you can,
> At all the times you can,
> To all the people you can,
> As long as ever you can."

1. Are we going on to perfection?

2. Do we expect to be made perfect in love in this life?

3. Are we earnestly striving after it?

Let us pray again:
"Eternal God, who commits to us the swift and solemn trust of life; since we know not what a day may bring forth, but only that the hour for serving you is always present, may we wake to the instant claims of your holy will; not waiting for tomorrow, but yielding today. Lay to rest, by the persuasion of your spirit, the resistance of our passion, indolence, or fear. Consecrate with your presence the way our feet may go, and the humblest work will shine, and the roughest places be made plain. Lift us above unrighteous anger and mistrust into faith and hope and charity by a simple and steadfast reliance on your sure will. In all things draw us to the mind of Christ, that your lost image may be traced again, and you may own us as at one with him and you. Amen."

James Martineau
Nineteenth-century British Unitarian leader

Remembering Jesus

Luke 24:13–32

"And they told what had happened on the road, and how he was known to them in the breaking of the bread."

I want to speak with you this morning about remembering Jesus. But I want to speak with you about remembering Jesus in two senses of the word "remembering." At my age we talk, and sometimes laugh, about our trouble remembering, like remembering where we put the car keys, and remembering what we were going to do when we walked from one room to another. This is remembering as a kind of mental activity, a bringing back into mind something we had in mind a few moments earlier.

But there is another meaning to the word "remember." It is related to how the apostle Paul spoke of the church as the body of Christ—as a body composed of many members, members who need one another to compose the whole body. To remember Jesus, in this case, means to put back together a body that has been broken apart, or taken apart, restoring something that has been *dis*membered. In this meaning of the word, to remember something is to restore to wholeness what belongs together.

I think it is important that we consider both these meanings as we gather at the table where Jesus told his disciples that as often as they break their bread or drink their wine that they remember him. As you eat each day, as you drink each day, "Remember me," he told them. "As often as you eat this bread and drink this cup, remember me."

From time to time, I read in the newspapers a story about a man or woman who has suffered a brain injury that produces what is called a global amnesia. The man does not remember his name. He does not remember if he is married or unmarried, if he has children or no children, if he has brothers or sisters or friends. In short, all those relationships that constitute his identity as a person are gone. His identity as a person is constituted by the memories of those relationships. Without those memories he does not know who he is, or what he is to do in his life.

In my own case "John Wesley" is the name my parents gave me. It is what they decided to call me. To explain who I am, I would tell you I am the son of Max and Dorothy Brown, the brother of Bernie, Maxine, and Beatrice, the father of Amy, Laurie, and Todd, grandfather to Nathan, Sarah, Alaina, Gabrielle, and great-grandfather to seven children whose names I have trouble recalling. I have been an ordained clergyman for sixty-three years with relationships with people in twelve congregations, and a college teacher for thirty of those years with relationships to hundreds of students and faculty colleagues.

Most central to my identity are memories of my relationship with people in and through the church, people who share with me the memory of Jesus, memories of who he was in the world, and who he continues to be in our lives.

When we come to the Lord's table, we are asked to remember Jesus. And as we remember Jesus, we restore the defining identity of our lives. We recall the relationship with him from whose love neither life nor death, nor angels, nor principalities, nor powers, nor height nor depth nor anything in the whole created order shall separate us. And as often as we take the bread and drink the cup, we not only remember Jesus, but we are called again to remember who we are, and whose we are, and what we are to be about in this world.

I think it is so important that the elements that Jesus blessed and broke at the table in that upper room in Jerusalem were the most common, the most available, the most daily foods of ordinary life. In attaching his memory to the most commonly experienced food of daily life the bread and wine were made symbols of the enduring grace of God in our lives. Bread. Wine. Food. God's presence. Here. Now. Remember me. Remember who you are.

I want to tell you a story. Sixty-four years ago, when I was a campus minister, I was asked to escort a group of thirty college students during Holy Week from the University of the Pacific to a work project in Tijuana, Mexico. The group was called Project Amigos, and its members had worked during that school year to raise money to fund their trip to work for a week at a social service center on the outskirts of Tijuana. We hired a bus to drive us overnight from Stockton, California, to Tijuana.

There were two buildings at this service center, buildings about the size of two Quonset huts. There was a water tap in one building but not in the other. There was one primitive outdoor toilet. The service center provided a medical clinic a few hours a week for that neighborhood, nursery care for children during certain hours of the day, a place for the community to gather for meetings. I remember there was a telephone there.

Across the street from the center was the community graveyard, colorful with green and red and yellow plastic flowers marking the many graves. I don't think there were any trees. There was no grass. Only the hard, sunbaked adobe earth that provided the roads, the walks, and the building blocks from which many homes were made.

From this graveyard we could look north from the hill we were on across the border to the United States, where we could see trees, lights, and, in the distance, the tall buildings of San Diego. Over there was home, water you could drink from a tap, a bed with a mattress, a phone you could use, a doctor you could call if you needed one, a stove you could cook on, and a refrigerator for your leftovers. Your life.

One task the students were asked to do was to dig a trench from one building to the next to connect a water line to the second building. Another task was to dig a septic system through the hard-baked adobe on the south side of that building—a large containment pit and drainage lines running south from it. This work required pick axes, pry bars, wedges, and shovels to break through the adobe. Just the kind of work young men love to do if there are lovely young women there to watch them do it. And some of the women were up to that work too, while others read to the nursery children, taught some English and learned some Spanish, helped the social center in its outreach to the community.

We all took turns cooking and washing up. There were no showers. We slept on the floors on air mattresses and sleeping bags we had brought. In the evenings we would sit in a circle and share with one another what we had learned about life in Tijuana that day, and what we had learned about ourselves that day. We learned a lot about ourselves, about who we were in the world, and what that might mean.

This was Holy Week, and so on Thursday evening we gathered to share our experience of the day. On the table was a plate of tortillas and a pitcher of Coca-Cola. Since we could not drink the water there, and since this was a Methodist youth group there could be no alcohol involved, tortillas and Coke were the elements we shared as we remembered Jesus, his teaching, his life, his death, his resurrected presence among his disciples. Through the most common food of that place, the body of Christ was remembered, remembered in every sense of that word. In that place, that evening, the body of Christ was remembered.

When we returned to University of the Pacific on Easter Sunday there was a new relationship among the Amigos, a new sense of identity among them. The Episcopal chaplain on campus was offended that we had celebrated the Lord's supper with tortillas and Coke. The Franciscan priest was thrilled and came to our home to offer Mass at our kitchen table.

Last year I received a letter from one of the Amigos. In the letter she shared the devotions she had led at choir practice at her church that week. She told about her experience with a group of students when she was in college that changed her life, that had made real the meaning of the body of Christ, broken and raised, a real presence in the world.

We, here, come from differing traditions in the church as we come to the Lord's table. What transcends all those differences is the commandment to remember Jesus. To remember Jesus is to recall that relationship that defines who we are in the world, and as we share the bread and the cup we re-member Jesus, restore and bring together the body of Christ to serve the world God loves.

Soul Food

Isaiah 55:1–11; I Corinthians 10:14–17

The point of my message this morning is pretty simple. It is this: You can never get enough of what you don't really want. I'll say it again, You can *never* get enough of what you don't really want.

It is a message that has been told in our religious tradition for more than three thousand years. Isaiah put it this way to his people living in Babylonian exile: "Why do you spend your money for that which is not bread, and your labor for that which does not satisfy?" Why indeed?

Here is how Jesus put it two thousand years ago, recorded in all three synoptic Gospels: "What does it profit a man if you gain the whole world and lose your soul?"

Saint Augustine put it this way seventeen hundred years ago, "You have made us for yourself, O God, and our souls are restless until they find their rest in thee."

Martin Luther said it this way: "The confidence and faith of the heart alone make both God and idol. That upon which you set your heart and put your trust is properly your god."

For three thousand years, the witness of the prophets and Jesus and the church has been that people—folks just like us—get distracted, get seduced, get fooled, get sold a bill of goods and buy the bread that does not really satisfy, or give us the time of our lives.

Why do people do this? Why do we do this? Maybe the answer is in the culture where we people live. Isaiah was writing to the Hebrews in Babylonian exile, that civilization with great military power, monumental architecture, and art. Paul was writing to the citizens of Corinth, that cosmopolitan crossroads of Greek and Roman religion and culture. Luther was writing toward the end of the European Renaissance, and he had been to Rome and had seen its glories in art and architecture.

Why do we spend our money for that which is not bread? Because we live in a culture that is rich and complex and distracting. *The Oregonian* boasts that Portland is now the destination for people who want wonderful places to eat, the new restaurant capital of America! We have a symphony, opera, theater, sports teams, parades, and dragon boat races.

We have shopping malls, more parks per capita than any other city in the USA. We have wine tours and hot-air balloon rides. We have Ducks and we have Beavers! We even have naked bike rides!

American advertising does everything it can to keep us from noticing that it is offering a material fix for our spiritual hunger. It does all it can to keep us from asking the one right question, What do I really want?

If we don't ask the right question, it doesn't really matter what answers the culture gives us—a new car, a new dress, new fingernails, a new pair of shoes. Did you know that the average number of pairs of shoes owned by an American woman is thirty-two? You would think that American women are people who walk everywhere.

But we don't walk. We drive! We own more automobiles per capita than any other country on earth. But 90 percent of the time each of our cars is parked! Indeed, in some metropolitan areas a place to park your car costs more than it does to drive it. And we know, or remember, what a soul-satisfying experience it is to drive in Portland, or on Interstate 405.

But the car ads would have us believe that owning a car means freedom, means fulfillment, means spiritually rejuvenating experiences in a beautiful wilderness. What's wrong with this picture? Have you driven your car lately?

Why do we spend our money on what is not bread? We do so because the advertising industry appeals to our human need to be accepted, to belong, to be esteemed, to feel that we are noticed, and feel that we are loved—all spiritual satisfactions, you will notice.

If marketers can keep us asking the wrong questions, it does not matter what answer the marketers give us. It will still be fast food, not soul food. We will still be setting our hearts and our hopes and our trust in those things that are not God at all.

Isaiah asks us a second question, "Why do we give our labor for that which does not satisfy?"

Why indeed? I don't often quote Sigmund Freud from the pulpit, but Freud was right when he said what a human being really needs to be happy is love and work. By love, Freud meant a physical and spiritual bond with other human beings, and by work, he meant activities that give us a sense that we are giving the time of our lives to a cause, to good purposes beyond ourselves.

Had Freud been writing theology rather than psychology he would have said what a human being needs to be happy is confidence in God's love, and to love what God loves, to be a part of a community that serves the purposes of God's love.

The message through the millennia of our tradition is that God loves the world, this world, the world that God declared to be good. As followers of Jesus, our faith communities are to be the agents of God's reconciling, saving, healing love in the world.

That is the purpose of a lifetime. That is a purpose that does not change no matter where we live or how old we are. To love what God loves is the calling of every Christian community.

There is a temptation for us to think that at our age we no longer can give our energies to love the world, to be participants in the reconciling love of God for the world. But Isaiah says, "Hearken diligently to me, and eat what is good—incline your ear to me; hear, that your soul may live."

We have among us, every day, people who are struggling with illness, with loneliness, with physical and emotional and mental challenges of many kinds. If you can dial a phone and say to your neighbor, "I have been thinking of you. Is there anything that you need?" "I'm praying for you. I'm going to the store. Is there something I can get for you?" "I'm coming to your neighborhood today—may I stop in and see how you're doing?" Your simple acts of thoughtful kindness make a loving, human connection in the world.

If we ourselves are in need and are humble and trusting enough to let our neighbors know, we are making room in their world for them to do a loving, meaningful task.

If we will recycle those material goods, those scraps from our abundant lives, we are loving the world God loves.

When we listen carefully to the words of our scriptures, what do we hear? What is it that God requires of us?

Not "Just do it!" But do justice—justice to the earth, justice to your neighbor. Not love attention but rather, "love kindness." Not "flaunt what you own," but rather, "walk humbly with your God."

There is a difference between fast food and soul food. One will fill your stomach and stuff your closets but leave you hungry. The other fills your heart and leaves you grateful and fulfilled.

You have made us for yourself, O God, and our souls are restless, our souls are hungry, until they find their rest in thee.

Eternal God, who gives to us the swift and solemn trust of life; since we know not what a day may bring, but only that the hour for serving you is always present, may we wake to the instant claims of your holy will; not waiting for tomorrow, but yielding today. Lay to rest, by the guidance of your spirit, the resistance of our passion, indolence, or fear. Consecrate with your presence the way our feet may go; and the humblest work will shine, and the roughest places be made plain. Lift us above unrighteous anger and mistrust into faith and hope and charity by a simple and steadfast reliance on your sure will. In all things draw us to

the mind of Christ, that your lost image may be traced again in us, and we may be at one with you and your creation.
Amen.
(James Martineau, revised)

It's Not Easy Being Green

Psalm 19, Romans 8:18–25

First United Church of Christ, Santa Barbara, July 15, 2001

I want to think with you for a few minutes this morning about frogs and faith. I am sure our congregation's resident naturalist and punner will think that when I join these two topics I am going to talk about some new leap of faith.

And perhaps, in a sense I am, for I want us to consider how our actions as a faith community may support or undermine the heavens and earth that "tell the glory of God," as our psalmist put it. I want us to consider how our actions prolong "the groaning of the whole creation," as Saint Paul put it, as we and all creation long for release from the futility that Paul saw characterizes all human activity that is contrary to the spirit of God. I hope we might come to share Paul's magnificent ecological vision, which sees the destiny of humankind bound together with the destiny of the whole creation.

But first, what about these frogs? If you have been reading the *Santa Barbara News-Press* these past few years you may be aware that the red-legged frog, whose habitat once extended from Mount Shasta to Baja California, and from the Sierra Nevada to the ocean, is now in danger of extinction. Federal laws now try to prevent the further human destruction of this creature's habitat so that it might have a chance to reproduce and to continue to contribute to the ecological balance of our countryside. And we must make no mistake, if it did not contribute to that balance, it would not have emerged and assumed a niche in our land's ecosystem.

Further, in Lassen, Yosemite, and Sequoia National Parks, biologists have noticed a ten-year decline in the population of the Yosemite toad and the yellow-legged frog. The biologists cite the unintended consequences of human activity—acid rain, increased ultraviolet radiation, warmer temperatures, and the drift of agricultural chemical sprays from the San Joaquin Valley ninety miles away—as contributing to the death of these little creatures.

When Jim Henson's lovable puppet, Kermit the Frog, sang to children gathered around their TV sets, "It's not easy being green," he did not know how truly he sang. For that little song is not merely a plea that we show empathy for human beings whose difference make them a target for discrimination and repression, but a plea for empathy toward all of God's creatures whose diversity proclaims the wonder and glory of the mysterious source of all being—of our own being.

But then the psalmist utters that startling phrase about his religious teachings: "Moreover, by them is your servant warned. But who can discover his errors? Clear thou me from hidden faults," he prays. "Keep back thy servant from presumptuous sins; let them not have dominion over me!"

What is the meaning of these "presumptuous sins?" What is this "dominion" they have over us?

According to my dictionary, to presume something is to take something for granted as true, without having proof to the contrary. For example, I presumed that if I stood up to speak this morning you would not immediately get up and walk out. I didn't know for sure that you wouldn't, but not having proof to the contrary, I stood up, intending to speak to you for about twenty minutes. To presume things, to organize complex actions regarding an unknown future, is a human spiritual capacity. It is rather like faith, in some respects.

I am presumptuous, on the other hand, if I presume too much. I am presumptuous if I engage in activities for which I have no authority or permission or adequate knowledge. Such presumptuous action may be arrogant and even offensive. If I presume to talk to you for forty minutes this morning, I am being presumptuous. I am presuming you have nothing better to do than listen to me talk, which is arrogant, even offensive.

Presumptuous sins, from which the psalmist prayed to be delivered, are those actions we undertake that are unwarranted given the state of our knowledge, which are arrogant, even offensive. Presumptuous sin is behavior that presumes too much because we know too little. Further, in the psalmist's understanding, the consequences of such activities boomerang, they come back to haunt us, or as he put it, they "have dominion over us." For example, consider this.

Draining the wetlands throughout my home state was presumed to be a good thing to do. After all, those wetlands could be put to better use raising corn and wheat. Or so my grandparents thought. But acting where they did not know, and not being able to foresee the consequences of their actions, they destroyed the nesting areas of birds and, thus, these natural predators of insects disappeared. This required the introduction of pesticides to control the insects. The wetland ponds were a natural water-filtering system. When they were destroyed, polluted water made its way across open ground, eroding the land over which it flowed taking pesticides with it. This necessitated the introduction of fertilizers, which themselves leached into wells, streams, and rivers. The loss of slowly released water from wetland ponds meant the decline of the feeder streams to major rivers, and this led to the loss of fish in those rivers and loss of wildlife that depends upon water for movement, for food, and for protection.

Now the counties in Minnesota compete for grants to try to restore wetlands, to reverse the consequences of our presumptuous ancestors.

But how could they have known? "Who can discover his errors?"

"Keep back thy servant from presumptuous sins; let them not have dominion over me."

Such examples of presumptuous human intrusion into the natural world abound in Africa, in Asia, in South America, in our country. I know you have heard of many of them. But their large number dramatizes the great dilemma we face in the twenty-first century: How do we overcome our alienation from the natural world? How do we reweave the web of life we have torn by our presumptuous doing?

But the very word "overcome" expresses what is the root of that alienation. We presume there is something "out there" we must overcome that will enable us to slip back into some mythical grove, some Eden out of which we have innocently wandered. But it is not that easy. It's not easy being green. Not easy at all!

The disruption of the natural world, daunting as it is, is the secondary problem. It is the consequence of the primary problem, the presumptuous sin of the human spirit acting in ignorance, acting without sufficient knowledge. Such action both expresses and perpetuates our alienation from the natural world. The problem is not, in the first instance, "out there." It is "in here," within us.

This is, of course, not a new insight. It is as old as the third chapter of Genesis. William Wordsworth put it this way in the middle of the nineteenth century:

"The world is too much with us: late and soon
getting and spending, we lay waste our powers.
Little we see in nature that is ours.
We have given our souls away! a sordid boon!"

Is there any good news this morning? Yes, possibly.

When we in the church are true to our understanding of the natural and spiritual dimensions of our lives we are, as an institution, at odds with the fundamental assumption of our culture.

In recent centuries the church has given itself over to a kind of disembodied spiritualism, to crusades to save souls that ignore our human rootedness in the natural world, and abandoned the natural world to presumptuous, arrogant, short-sighted behavior.

We human beings managed very well for thousands of years without Styrofoam and the throw-away plastic our culture shoves at us. We still can!

It's not easy being green. Our church needs to withdraw from presumptuous consumption. Is our landscaping drought-tolerant, environmentally responsible? Is our heating and lighting energy-efficient? Is the remodeling of the fellowship hall going to be environmentally responsible in the materials we use? Are we willing to take the little time it takes to wash our cups on Sunday morning, rather than adding Styrofoam to the landfill? If we aren't willing, who will be?

It's not easy being green. But I urge this congregation to study and adopt the environmental covenant being proposed by the United Church of Christ and other denominations. It should already be on the agenda for Church Council.

I am becoming presumptuous in the length of this sermon. Let me close with an appeal to you to hear again Paul's words. "The creation waits with eager longing for the revealing of the children of God."

It is not easy being green, but discerning the ways of God in the world is a path to fulfillment and meaning, "reviving the soul, making wise the simple, rejoicing the heart, enlightening the eyes. It is true and righteous altogether."

Amen.

Natural Righteousness

Psalm 19

Last year about this time I agreed to read grant proposals for the Ecumenical Ministries of Oregon Pollinator Project. Among the fifteen proposals submitted was one from the congregation called Kairos United Church of Christ. I was really impressed with the grant proposal and went to the Kairos UCC website to learn more about this congregation. I was really impressed with what I read on the website and determined to visit this interesting, socially engaged, worshipping community one Sunday. My wife and I came one Sunday, and by the end of the service I had a feeling that I had come to a warm home after a long, long journey among God's frozen people. I heard a preacher who avoided stained-glass language and spoke the truth of his own experience as a human being living the Gospel of Jesus.

I found people who are more interested in living the Gospel than arguing about doctrinal differences. And I heard musicians who know that beauty is one of the pathways to God, and that music expresses and touches the depths of the human soul in ways that words alone cannot do.

So, I want, first of all, to say thank you to the Green Committee, the Kairos musicians, and this community. Thank you for who you are and for what you are doing in the world.

I want to speak this morning about a much misunderstood and

much abused word in our theological tradition and how recovery of the meaning of that word can help us understand who we are and what we are supposed to be about in this world—especially what we are to be about in the days we have ahead of us to reverse the destruction caused by climate change.

The word is "righteousness." It is a word that feels strange in my mouth because it is so little used these days. I grew up in a Methodist parsonage in North Dakota thinking that to be a righteous person meant not doing most of the things my friends at school did—not dance, not play cards, not go to movies on Sunday, certainly not sneak a beer behind the grandstand, or sneak a smoke outside the ice-skating rink.

It wasn't until I started to study the Bible in college that I learned that being righteous is a term that has to do with the quality of our relationships. Righteous living is about maintaining the proper relationship with God and with all that God loves. And central to the message of the Gospel of Jesus is that God loves the world.

I might have figured out sooner what a righteous life is if I had understood the Hebrew language. If I had known Hebrew, I would have known that after God declared all creation to be good, God told Adam and Eve that they were to have dominion over all the creatures of the earth. To "have dominion" means that they were to govern the earth as God's stewards, to act as God's agents, to fulfill God's intention for the whole creation that God had declared good. That was their righteous relationship, their proper relationship to God and creation.

If I had known Hebrew, I would have known that when God told Noah to take the animals into the ark and "to keep them alive with you" the Hebrew form of the verb translated "to keep them alive with you" is a causative construction. God's instruction to Noah could as well be translated as "cause them to continue to live with you." And as if to emphasize the point, at the end of the flood, God's instruction to Noah was "to bring out with you every living thing that is with you of all flesh—birds, and animals, and everything that creeps upon the earth so that they may abound on the earth and be fruitful and multiply on the earth" (Gen. 8:17). To cause the diversity of life to continue with humankind—that was the righteous relationship between God, Noah, and the animal world.

If I had grown up knowing Hebrew, I might have been more attuned to the meaning of Psalm 19, which I read a few moments ago. The whole of creation displays the glory of God. There are no words or any voice that can adequately make this point. But just look! Just listen! Just attend to the marvel and the mystery of the world above and around you. This, says the psalmist, is what we have been given dominion over, to be responsible for it and not to destroy it.

There is a legal term that describes this righteous relationship between human beings and the world God has given into our care. The legal term is "usufruct." To be given a usufruct means to be given the use of something that belongs to another (in this case to God) to use and to enjoy so long as it is not destroyed or injured by our use of it.

The gift of this world is so great! And the responsibility of this gift is no less great! No wonder the psalmist follows his exaltation in the beauty of creation with a reminder of the wise, guiding, soul-reviving precepts of the commandments of God. The temptations of human greed are so powerful! Our human inclination to rationalize, to find pleasing reasons for our bad behavior, are so strong! The psalmist knows this and cries: "Who can detect their errors? Clear Thou me from hidden faults. Keep back your servant from presumptuous sins. Do not let them have dominion over me. Then I shall be blameless and innocent of great transgression" (Psalm 19:12–13).

Clearly, the psalmist wants to live a righteous life, to avoid the obvious violations of his relationship with God. But he also wants to avoid what he calls "presumptuous sin." Now there is a curious idea, "presumptuous sins." What could the psalmist mean by this?

According to my dictionary, to presume something is to take something for granted, to believe something because you have no proof to the contrary. For example, I presumed that you would be here this morning. I did not know for sure that you would be here, but I prepared this sermon in the presumption that you would be. Being able to presume things, to act with regard to an unknown future, is a human capacity something like faith, actually.

I am presumptuous, on the other hand, if I presume too much. I am presumptuous if I engage in activities for which I have no authority, or no permission, or no competence. I am presumptuous if I plan to talk for sixty minutes, rather than twenty minutes, expecting that you have nothing better to do than sit and listen to me. Presumptuous sins are those actions we undertake heedless of the consequences of our actions, actions that are unwarranted given the state of our knowledge. Presumptuous sin is behavior that presumes too much, because we know too little.

Furthermore, in the psalmist's understanding, the consequences of such actions boomerang, they come back to haunt us, or, in his words, they come back to rule us, to "have dominion over us." "Save me from presumptuous sins, let them not have dominion over me."

If there were a scriptural basis for the worldwide environmental movement, it would be Psalm 19. The catalog of presumptuous sins of the last three hundred years is a long one. It would take more than fifty minutes just to list them. Is it too much of a stretch to see that when righteousness came to be identified with personal, individual piety—about keeping one's own moral scorecard in order—something tragic began to take place in the larger world around us?

The pietism of our Puritan and Methodist ancestors coincided with the beginning and development of the Industrial Revolution, and continued through the eighteenth, nineteenth and twentieth centuries. Being materially successful became a sign of God's blessing. Bigger barns meant bigger blessings. Dominion over the earth meant using it for the benefit of one species—our own. And so we filled the air we all breathe with the smoke of coal and oil and we became rich. We turned the rivers and streams into waste disposal systems, and we considered not at all the cost to all other creatures that dwell in and use those waters.

And the consequences of our presumptuous sins—our unrighteous relationships with the natural world of which we are a part—are having dominion over us. The disappearance of the world's glaciers due to global warming means the end of irrigation in the countries of Asia that depend on the rivers flowing out of the Himalayas for water to drink, as well as to irrigate their crops. Where will the millions of people of Asia find water? Where will the millions of people of Asia find food? What will become of all forms of life that depend upon waters that flow from those mountains?

Here in Oregon and in California we are now asking the same question as snowpack and glaciers retreat from the Sierra and Cascade ranges. "Save Thou me from presumptuous sins, let them not have dominion over me." And the acidification of the ocean and decline of those minute species in the ocean at the base of the food chain in our seas. And dynamiting the tops off the mountains of Appalachia to get at coal, and the erosion of hillsides and the pollution of the whole watershed? We all live downwind and downstream from our unsustainable industries.

Save us, Oh God, from presumptuous sins, let them not have dominion over us.

Then there is the loss of pollinator insects that threatens food production in the agricultural valleys of California and Oregon. This on top of droughts caused by climate disruption. Here in the United States our removal and replacement of native plants has destroyed the food source that native insects require for food. The insects do not recognize, cannot chew, and cannot digest plants with which they did not evolve. When the plants that insects evolved with are gone, the native insects die out. And the loss of native insects means the loss of bird species, because birds require those insects to feed their baby birds. The loss of baby birds means the end of adult birds. No more babies, no more birds. We are losing bird species every year. I am sure we did not know that when we replaced native plants of Oregon with ornamentals from Asia or Iowa.

Save us, O God, from presumptuous sins, let them not have dominion over us.

In its 2013 annual report, the Oregon Nature Conservancy points out that 70 percent of Oregonians live within twenty miles of the banks of the Willamette River. It reports that 85 percent of the Willamette River floodplain has been lost to development. The report is talking about us and about where we live.

This is the context for the Kairos United Church of Christ pollinator project. Plants that are native to the Willamette Valley watershed are crucial to the restoration of biodiversity where we live. It is plants that turn sunlight into green tissue for insects, and into oxygen for every creature that has lungs. It is these plants that are needed by every living thing native to this place—birds, mammals, everything that creeps upon the earth—so that they may abound on the earth and be fruitful and multiply on the earth.

The Kairos Pollinator Project can be a living, growing, actual and symbolic expression of the righteous life of this community of faith. It does not need to be just a small step. It might be just the first step. It might become an anchor, or a wayside stop on a pollinator pathway that extends the length of Logus Road or connects us to Johnson Creek and the Springwater Trail. It might become a pollinator pathway that, in time, defines this neighborhood in Portland.

Marc McGinnes founded the Environmental Defense Center in Santa Barbara in response to the disastrous oil well blowout in the Santa Barbara Channel in 1969. That was an environmental disaster that catalyzed the modern environmental movement. He was asked this question, "How do you keep from being overcome by despair and fear when you see what we have done to the planet on which we live?"

Marc said: "Love is the most powerful force on earth. When you truly love something, you get past despair, you get past your fear, you act to save that which you love." He went on to say: "Environmentalism is a spiritual discipline. It comes from humility about our place in the procession of life. It arises from gratitude for the earth on which we live. Before I can go to work each day, I have to go outside, I look at this marvelous, beautiful place in which I live, and I am grateful—I am amazed—I am humbled. Then I can go to work to try and save this place I love."

Here is a prayer for such a spiritual discipline:

i thank You God for most this amazing
day: for the leaping greenly spirits of trees
and a blue true dream of sky; and for everything
which is natural which is infinite which is yes
I who have died am alive again today,
and this is the sun's birthday; this is the birth
day of life and of love and wings: and of the gay
great happening illimitably earth
how should tasting touching hearing seeing
breathing any-lifted from the no
of all nothing—human merely being
doubt unimaginable You?
(now the ears of my ears awake and now the eyes of my eyes are opened)
—E. E. Cummings

Amen.

A Faithful Ecology

Psalm 19, Matthew 6:24–33

Preached July 9, 2023, at First United Methodist Church, Eugene, Oregon

When your pastor asked if I would be willing to preach this Sunday, I began to think about how the Christian Church can respond to the environmental disasters that are the consequence of climate change. I thought I would begin with whatever disaster was most recent, since this would most likely be the one most on our minds. But in the past three weeks there have been heat domes over the Southwest, temperatures above 110 degrees in Texas, tornadoes across the Midwest, weeks of smoky air pollution from the East Coast all the way to North Dakota from wildfires burning in Canada. The glaciers in the Himalayan mountains that feed the rivers of India are melting, endangering the food supply for millions of people living there.

The most recent disaster? Where should I begin?

Last week I received a sixty-page article from the Post Carbon Institute titled "The Great Unraveling." The article documents the current situation on this planet that can be attributed to the land use practices and the use of fossil fuels to energize the world economies—the very practices by which modern societies organize and sustain themselves.

The Post Carbon Institute describes how, worldwide, the social, economic, and political fabric of societies is unraveling. This situation has resulted in the average population size of vertebrate animals, (including mammals, fish, birds, amphibians, and reptiles) declining by 69 percent in just the past fifty years. In addition, currently around two billion people lack access to safe drinking water. Further, by the year 2050 demand for water will have grown by 40 percent, and 25 percent of the world's people will live in countries without sufficient access to clean water.

In the last five pages of the Post Carbon Institute's report, it proposes what people like us can do now to prepare for a future that none of us imagined when we were growing up. How can we become resilient communities in the face of such environmental threats?

Where can we begin? What steps must we be taking now?

I believe this congregation has already begun to take the right steps in its programs of social outreach in this community. We can provide shelter, warmth, cooling, food, and safety for strangers in our community. We do these things because of the teaching of our religious heritage. And I believe that with a fuller understanding of our creation stories, and a more inclusive understanding of Jesus's message about the Kingdom of God, we will better prepare to meet the multiple challenges we face with climate change. It is these two things I want to speak about this morning.

Let us begin with our creation stories. Michael Rosenzweig is a professor of ecology and evolutionary biology at the University of Arizona. In his book *Win Win Ecology*, Rosenzweig points out that in the Genesis story of the Garden of Eden, God declares all creation to be good. In the story, God tells Adam and Eve that they are to have dominion over all the creatures of the earth. However, Rosenzweig points out that in the Hebrew language, in which the Genesis story was written, the word that is translated "dominion" in English Bibles is the same word used to describe how a shepherd cares for its sheep. God's charge to Adam—that is, to all humankind—to us—is to care for the earth as does a shepherd care for his and her sheep. That is the charge given to Adam and Eve, to all men and women in the Genesis creation story. Taking care of the creatures of the earth is our task as human beings, and our proper relationship to God and creation. The word "dominion" just doesn't cut it.

Furthermore, Rosenzweig points out, that in the story of the great flood when God told Noah to take the animals into the ark and "to keep them alive with you," the Hebrew form of the verb translated "to keep them alive with you" is a causative construction. God's instruction to Noah could be more accurately translated as "cause them to continue to live with you." And as if to emphasize the point, at the end of the flood story, God's instruction to Noah is "to bring out with you every living thing that is with you of all flesh—birds, and animals, and everything that creeps upon the earth—so that they may abound on the earth and be fruitful and multiply on the earth" (Gen. 8:17). To cause the diversity of life to continue with humankind—that was the righteous relationship between God, Noah, and the animal world.

Now, contemporary ecological studies emphasize the interdependence of plant and animal species. No insects—no pollination. No pollination—no plants. No plants—no food and no oxygen. No oxygen, no more life.

To cause the diverse life to continue on earth must include the diversity of plants on earth upon which all forms of animal life depend. That is the divine purpose given to us men and women in the origin story of our faith tradition.

If I had grown up knowing Hebrew, I might have been more attuned to the meaning of Psalm 19, which I read a few moments ago. The whole creation displays the glory of God. There are no words or any voice that can adequately make this point. But just look! Just listen! Just attend to the marvel and the mystery of the world above us and around us. This, says the psalmist, is our righteous relationship to the creation, to attend to it, to learn from it, to respond to it. Not to destroy it.

It is a way of living in the world that preindustrial societies and indigenous peoples on this land practiced for centuries before being colonized by European nations. It is a way of living that does not exclude human beings from the natural world. The natural world is the world in which we humans evolved. We might notice that in the Genesis story human beings appear in the Garden of Eden only after the garden has been created.

The presumptuous sin which the psalmist prays to be saved from is that we humans act like we are exempt from the conditions of what we call "the natural world." That is presumptuous of us. The suffering and death brought about by climate change demonstrate that we are not exempt from but very much a part of the natural world.

Marc McGinnes founded the Environmental Defense Center in Santa Barbara in response to the disastrous oil well blowout in the Santa Barbara Channel in 1969. That was an environmental disaster that catalyzed the modern environmental movement. Marc was asked this question, "How do you keep from being overcome by despair and fear when you see what we have done to the planet on which we live?" Mark said: "Love is the most powerful force on earth. When you truly love something, you get past despair, you get past your fear, you act to save that which you love." He went on to say, "Environmentalism is a spiritual discipline."

Now, Jesus was not what we today call an ecologist. But Jesus was, nonetheless, an astute observer of what we call the "natural world." Jesus told his followers: Consider the lilies of the field. Consider the birds of the air. Jesus did go into the wilderness to restore his spirit, to renew his vision, to experience the love of God, which he saw and felt all around him in the natural world. Jesus warned his followers not to mistake material wealth for the blessing of God. Bigger barns do not equate to bigger blessings.

During the nine years I lived in a retirement community in Milwaukie, Oregon, I saw two huge buildings being built. Each one filled a whole city block. The purpose of the buildings was called "self-storage." What a strange and tragic idea—a building for "self-storage." Do we identify our self with stuff? In our mercantile world of advertising, I am afraid we do. Are we more known by the stuff we own than by the deeds we do?

Jesus could well have said, "You can never get enough of what you don't really need." He did say: "You fool. This night your soul is required of you. You cannot serve God and mammon"—living to get more stuff.

Jesus's message is that the Kingdom of God is both a personal experience and a social reality. We experience the reign of God as persons in a community of loving people. In his parable of the last judgment, Jesus made it clear that when all is said and done, it is what we do for one another, and for the least of those around us, that really matters—not what we own or what we say we believe. Feed the hungry, welcome the stranger, visit the lonely. And if we are to feed the hungry, we must care for the plants of the earth, because it is the plants of the earth upon which all life forms depend for their sustenance.

We have been making a presumptuous mistake to speak of the Kingdom of God as one thing and the plant kingdom as if it were something else. The Kingdom of God is not just the community of humans. The Kingdom of God is a personal experience of the whole Garden of Eden.

As a community of Christians, we have a heritage and a commission to attend to. Our scriptures charge us to care for the natural world with the attention and concern as do shepherds for their flocks. And we are charged to love one another, to feed the hungry, to welcome the stranger, to love our neighbor as ourselves.

And as we experience the consequences of our failures to shepherd the plants and animals of what we call the natural world, we will need—even more—to build in this place a loving, caring, supportive, ministering community of the Kingdom of God. We are called to enact a faithful ecology of the Kingdom of God.

I pray we may do so together as a congregation, in this community and in this space.

Here is a prayer for such a faithful ecology:

i thank You God for most this amazing day:
for the leaping greenly spirits of trees
and a blue true dream of sky; and for everything
which is natural which is infinite which is yes
(i who have died am alive again today,
and this is the sun's birthday; this is the birth
day of life and of love and wings: and of the gay
great happening illimitably earth)
how should tasting touching hearing seeing
breathing any—lifted from the no
of all nothing—human merely being
doubt unimaginable You?
(now the ears of my ears awake and
now the eyes of my eyes are opened)

Amen, and thank you God for E. E. Cummings.

EASTER

Easter. Again.

Luke 24:1–12 and 1 Corinthians 12:27

SERMON FOR KAIROS UCC, 2019

"Now you are the body of Christ and individually members of it."

As I was thinking about this service, I began to imagine what it was like for those first disciples of Jesus that evening of the first Easter. Jesus, just seven days before, had been welcomed into the Holy City—Jerusalem—the city now governed by the imperial power of Rome. He had been greeted by crowds of people shouting "hosanna" in the streets. "Hosanna!" The word does not mean "hip, hip, hooray!" The word "hosanna" means "Save us, save us now."

The people were celebrating the Passover, celebrating the Hebrew peoples' escape from Egyptian slavery. But their Holy City was now occupied by Roman soldiers under Roman rule.

The disciples remembered Jesus who had eaten and prayed with them in the garden of Gethsemane just three nights before. Jesus, who had been their teacher and companion as they traveled together through the villages of Galilee. Jesus! Their leader. Their friend. Now publicly crucified. They had watched him suffer. They had watched him die. They had seen it with their own eyes. Imagine their fear. Imagine their grief. Imagine their confusion.

"What are we to do now? Where can we go now? Rome is still the imperial power here. We believed Jesus was the long-awaited Messiah, the Christ. But he's dead. If Jesus was the Christ—the

Messiah—then the game is all over. No more Messiah to wait for. We're done. We're finished. It's over. There is no reason to hope. If we go back into the villages of Galilee teaching Jesus is the Messiah, the people will laugh at us, and the Romans will crucify us, just as surely as they did him."

Yes, Jesus's mother and Mary Magdalene and the other women had come to them and told them that the tomb was empty. But as we read in Luke's Gospel this morning, "These words seemed to them to be an idle tale, and they did not believe them" (Luke 24:1-12). They had not been to the tomb. They had not experienced the resurrection of Jesus.

Remember, on that first Easter evening there was no Gospel of Luke, no Gospel of Matthew, no Gospel of Mark, or Gospel of John. The stories of Jesus's crucifixion, burial, and resurrection would not be written for another fifty years. There was no Book of the Acts of the Apostles—for they were the apostles and they had not acted yet! They believed they had no reason to act! The future they had counted on was no future at all. They had to imagine a whole new future, not only for themselves but for their whole nation!

Have you had that experience? The realization that the life you had hoped to live has become impossible to live. That the future you had assumed was yours would not be yours, could not be yours, or your children's or your grandchildren's world. That nothing about your future was certain. That you could not even count on the seasons of the year to be what they had been for as long as anyone could remember.

As I think about the experience of those first followers of Jesus, I find something very similar in the lives of people today who see the tempests, the tornadoes, the fires, the floods, the hurricanes, the droughts, and the millions of people made refugees by famine. The oceans are rising, driving island residents from their homes. The oceans, so vast, so deep, changed by the pollution produced by the way we humans have been living.

Children are marching in the streets and crying out: "Our house is on fire! The planet is burning!" Hosanna—save us!

How did we get to this situation? Where did we go so wrong? To whom do we turn for direction? How did we get from the joy of Easter to the despair of climate change? And how might we recover that joy? It is a long story, but here are two important chapters in that story.

First, in the Hebrew creation story (Gen. 1:26) we read that Adam—the name is a plural noun meaning "all men"—was given the honor and responsibility to name and to care for the creatures of the earth. The English translation of that direction has been—tragically—the word "dominion." Dominion over the creatures of the earth. But the word translated "dominion" is the same Hebrew word used to describe a shepherd's care for his or her flock. In our creation story we humans were charged to care for the creatures of the earth, to know them, and to name them, to look after the creatures of the earth as good shepherds would care for their sheep. That is the role given humans in the Eden story. "Dominion," on the other hand, carries the notion of imperial ownership.

The idea found in Genesis that human beings are the stewards, the shepherds, the caretakers of God's world was instituted in Roman secular law with the term "usufruct." In the law, a usufruct is defined as "the right of enjoying all the advantages derivable from the use of something that belongs to another, as far as is compatible with the substance of the thing not being destroyed or injured."

In plain language: "You may use it, so long as you don't abuse it." The psalmist sang: "The earth is the Lord's, *and* the fullness thereof." The instruction to humans is to care for God's creation. The earth is our usufruct, it is ours to use and enjoy as far as is compatible with "it not being destroyed or injured."

The air, the wind, the sun, rivers, the tides, the soil, are gifts of the earth, free for our use so long as we do not destroy or injure them.

But in our culture, we developed the idea of "dominion," of private ownership, that we own the earth. The earth is our property to use however we want. The old-growth forest on the east flank of Mount Hood is just so many board feet of lumber! We built a legal system and an economic system that protects the idea that the earth is just full of stuff that we can own. Blowing the tops off mountains and pumping chemicals into the depth of the ground so we can bring up fossil fuels is our legal right. And we have poisoned the rivers and the air by our actions, all for the sake of making more money, more stuff, for which we need bigger barns, and bigger and bigger barns. And all the while the creatures of the earth are going extinct because of our actions.

About such actions Jesus said: "Thou fool! Thou fool! This night your soul is required of you. Do not lay up treasures on earth where they rot and corrupt. Seek the kingdom of heaven, the reign of God, and what you really need will be provided."

Put in contemporary language: We can never get enough of what we don't really need, and the pursuit of those things that we don't really need is destroying the world God has entrusted to our care.

Now, getting back to Easter. Before the first Easter week was over the disciples had experienced the risen Christ. The good news that the love of God never ends, that Jesus is the Christ, that the love that brought all worlds into being is not defeated by death, and the body of Christ—the fellowship of believers—is charged to be the loving hearts, the learning minds, the physical strength, and the agents to express God's love and care for the world.

Wherever the spirit of the Lord is, there is the body of Christ in the world.

We are this morning called to continue Christ's ministry of love, of redemption, of reconciliation, of healing in the world, to make a difference in the world.

In the face of the crises that human greed, pride, and egotism have brought about we need to imagine a social order not based on endless consumption in a finite world, but one based on an infinite love in and beyond all worlds. We are to be agents of God's love of the earth, love of our neighbor, love of a social order where the hungry are fed, the thirsty find water, the naked are clothed, the stranger is welcomed, the sick find healing, and the prisoner finds loving human companionship.

We need a moral imagination that informs our politics, our economics, our daily lives. But it is not really a new moral imagination. The images are there in our religious traditions, in our creation stories, there in the judgment of our prophets who call us to do justice on the earth, to love kindness, to walk humbly.

There is that remarkable story in the fourth chapter of the Book Acts that tells how the followers of Jesus came together to share all that they owned so that there were no needy persons among them (Acts 4:32). The histories of the Roman Empire describe the early Christians as remarkable people because they cared for the sick and ministered to the hungry when epidemics swept through the crowded cities.

There are other examples of indigenous communities in which all virtues begin with gratitude—gratitude for the gifts of the natural world, this beautiful, bountiful earth where we walk in beauty as the miracle of life itself, receiving what we really need, but not taking more than we can really use.

As Paul told the followers of Jesus in his letter to them in Corinth (1 Cor 12:27), "Now you are the body of Christ and individually members of it." And as the body has many different members, each with its own gifts and purposes, even so, this body—this community—is blessed with rich and diverse gifts in our own lives and experiences.

We are the body of Christ, the community of the resurrection in this place. Each Sunday is Easter again, the beginning of a new Earth Week in our country, and for us again to remember and to act each day as stewards of God's creation.

May we begin each new day with gratitude.

Gratitude for the gift of life and the gift of purpose for our lives.

May we arise each day to another day of loving.

Each new day an Easter! Again!

"Christ of the Commonplace"

Easter Sunrise Service

Luke 24:13–35

The story of these two followers of Jesus on the road to Emmaus is one of the strangest stories recorded by the early church about its experience with Jesus the Messiah. If it were not for the wonderful conclusion, the recognition of Jesus in the breaking of bread, the story might almost be a case study in the foolishness of Jesus's followers.

Just look at the story. Two people, one of them a man named Cleopas, the other wholly anonymous, whether a man or a woman, we don't know, are leaving Jerusalem on the very day the resurrection of Jesus has been reported. Right off the bat, doesn't that seem a little bit strange? If you were a follower of the person you believed to be the Messiah, the one destined to save your people from the crushing oppression of Rome, and you were told that although he had been executed publicly as a subversive criminal three days before, and that he was now seen, alive, in Jerusalem—don't you think you might have decided to stay in Jerusalem in the hopes of seeing him again?

Well, these two didn't. For some reason they are leaving Jerusalem on a seven-mile hike to Emmaus. Maybe they lived there. Maybe they had work they had to get home to. Maybe they were going to stay with friends since Jerusalem was probably terribly crowded with pilgrims for the Passover celebration. We don't know why they were going to Emmaus. We only know they were going from the place where Jesus had been reported raised from death to life. Well, OK.

Then this stranger comes up to them as they are walking along, and he hears them talking about all the events of the past three days, hears them discussing Jesus's death and the reports that his tomb was found empty that morning. So, the stranger asks them: "What's up? What are you talking about?"

"Oh," says Cleopas, looking sad, "you must be the only person in Jerusalem who doesn't know what has happened." (How is that for irony!)

"Really," says the stranger. "What things? Tell me about them!" (How is that for generosity!)

So, Cleopas and his friend tell the story, how they had hoped that Jesus of Nazareth was the one who would set their nation free but that religious and political leaders had conspired to kill him and had, indeed, crucified him three days earlier. And now some women of their group had told them this morning that his tomb was empty, that angels had told them Jesus was alive, that the men had checked out the story that the tomb was empty, but they hadn't seen Jesus.

This is really discouraging to the stranger. (Why wouldn't it be!) "Oh, how foolish you are. How slow you are to believe everything your tradition should have taught you!" And the stranger gives them a history lesson, right back to the founding of their nation by Moses, in order to put the life of the Messiah into proper perspective.

And Cleopas and his friend still don't get it!

So, when they get near to Emmaus, the stranger begins to walk off and leave them. (You can well imagine why he might want to!) But the two say: "Listen, friend, it's late. It will soon be dark. Come stay with us in town. It has been a long day. Let's get something to eat."

So, they find a place to eat, and the stranger picks up the loaf of bread, he asks for God's blessing upon the sharing of this meal. He breaks the bread and gives it to them. And then, and only then, they recognize that the risen Christ is with them.

And as they recognize him, he vanishes!

And Cleopas and his friend say: "You know, that really was a great sermon he gave us on the road back there. Yes, I can sure see it now! It was like my heart was on fire." So, they get up from the table and immediately make the seven-mile hike back to Jerusalem in the dark. They tell the other disciples about the stranger they met on the road, and how they finally recognized Jesus when they broke bread together.

Luke's Gospel is the only Gospel that records this story. Mark's Gospel, in two verses, says there was a report of Jesus appearing to two people who were walking in the country, but the disciples didn't believe their story (Mark 9:12-13).

Why would the early church preserve this story? Why would Luke, alone, preserve this story in his Gospel? It certainly doesn't show Cleopas and his nameless companion to be particularly discerning people! It doesn't show them to be particularly clever. It doesn't show them to be particularly devoted to Jesus; after all, they are headed out of town on the day of his resurrection! It doesn't show them to be interpersonally sensitive, spending an afternoon with a stranger and not even learning his name.

It does show them to be believers who were all wrapped up in their own concerns, looking sad but not so broken up that they couldn't carry on a good discussion while walking to Emmaus.

It does show them, nonetheless, as decent people who eventually remember their manners and invite the stranger who has shared the journey with them to stop and share a meal with them as well.

It shows them as believers who recognized a good sermon when they heard it, but who couldn't repeat what they heard or what they experienced in a way that convinced the folks back in Jerusalem of the reality of their experience.

You know, they sound a lot like me, this Cleopas and his anonymous friend, so wrapped up in the affairs of the day that I don't recognize the grace of God's love as I walk down the road of life, slow to learn, slower to share!

This may well be why the church preserved this story, a story not about sunrise at the tomb but a story about an afternoon in the experience of believers when the news of the risen Christ has spread, and the followers are trying to decide what it all means. Clearly, the story is the church saying that disciples recognize the risen Christ in the blessing and breaking of bread. It is then that we see the living Christ among us.

But do we? Do we really?

Our scriptures are filled with stories of the grace of God being experienced in the ordinary events and ordinary relationships of life. David and Jonathan—God's grace in human friendship; Ruth and Naomi—God's grace in the loyalty of the extended family; the child Samuel and the elder Eli—God's grace in the respect and love between generations; Mary and Joseph—God's grace in the midst of married life; Jesus at the wedding in Canna—God's grace in the celebration of human love.

These scriptures tell us that it is not the otherworldly and miraculous that mediate to us the wonder of God's love. It is in the common places of life that God meets us with the gifts of grace, and if we do not recognize that truth here, now, in the daily occurrence of our life, we are not apt to recognize it in the onetime occurrence of Easter.

We were raised to life this morning when we awoke into consciousness in this incredible, mysterious, marvelous world. Shall we recognize the risen Christ if we cannot recognize the unlikely miracle of our own existence, given anew to us each morning?

Shall we see the love of God in an event two thousand years ago if we are blind to the love and grace of God we know daily from our spouse, our children, our sisters, our brothers, our friends?

According to Matthew's Gospel, Jesus's last words to his disciples were, "Remember, I am with you always, to the very end of the age." I am with you always, even on the Emmaus road. I am with you always, even as the sun shines brightly at Friendship Park this morning.

Shall I recognize the miracle of Easter morning if I am blind to the marvel—of every morning?

I don't think so. If I am unable to recognize the love of God in the breaking of bread in a community of friends, how shall I ever recognize the love of God in the broken seal on an empty tomb?

The poet E. E. Cummings gave us this prayer for Easter morning:

> I thank You God for most this amazing
> day: for the leaping greenly spirits of trees
> and a blue true dream of sky; and for everything
> which is natural which is infinite which is yes
>
> (i who have died am alive again today,
> and this is the sun's birthday; this is the birth
> day of life and of love and wings: and of the gay
> great happening illimitably earth)
>
> how should tasting touching hearing seeing
> breathing any—lifted from the no
> of all nothing—human merely being
> doubt unimaginable You?
>
> (now the ears of my ears awake and
> now the eyes of my eyes are opened)

Christ is risen! Thanks be to God!

PENTECOST

This sermon was preached during the Wednesday morning worship service held in the twenty-four-hour care center at the Rose Villa Retirement Community in Milwaukie, Oregon. The weekly service of song, prayer, and meditation was sponsored by the United Christian Fellowship of Rose Villa.

Being the Church

John 1:1–18

This morning I want to think with you for a few minutes about what it means to be the church. I suspect that most of us who are here this morning have been members of the church in different places where we have lived. I want you to know that you are just as much members of the church where you are living now as you ever were when you were living somewhere else.

As you know, English can be a confusing language. And one of the confusions is the way it confuses how we talk about the church.

For example, if I say that I am going to go to San Francisco, you will understand that I am going away, going to someplace where I am not right now. If I say I am going to Fred Meyer's, you will know that I am not there right now and will need to leave where I am right now in order to go to Fred Meyer's.

Because we speak the English language this way, when I say, "I am going to church," we think that it means we have to go somewhere else other than where we are right now. It gets us thinking that the church is a place—a building at some other *place*—instead of the church being the persons we are anyplace we are, and everyplace we are.

When the apostle Paul wrote his letters to Rome, and Corinth, and Ephesus, he wasn't writing to a building with a street address, he was writing to the people living in Corinth, to people in Ephesus, and Rome, and people in all of Galatia who had come to know the love of God through his preaching and teaching about Jesus. He did not tell them to, "Go to the church." Rather, he counsels them on how it is they can be the church. So, let's think together for a few moments about what it means to be the church.

The first thing to be said is that what distinguishes the church from other people is that the church is a worshipping community. As we worship, we open our imperfect lives to the instruction and the compassionate love of God who loves and sustains us from day to day. It is as a worshipping community we know ourselves to be people called to love God and the world God loves—with all our heart and all our mind and all our strength. We gather as a community of imperfect people who are seeking to walk the path of love and forgiveness that Jesus walked. It is a path that welcomes people of every age, of every color, of every gender, of every nation, of every age as children of the God Jesus called, "Abba," Father.

We live in a world where people worship power, where people worship money, where people worship and devote their lives to whatever cultural idol says they must have if they are to be respected, if they are to be loved, if they are to matter in the world.

But the church at worship listens to a different voice, responds to a different call: "Come unto me all you who are weak and heavy laden, and I will give you rest. Take my yoke upon you and learn of me, for my yoke is easy, and my burden is light."

How desperately our world needs to heed such a call, to be such a community, such a family. At worship we hear the apostle Paul counsel us to, "Let all bitterness, and wrath, and anger, clamor, and evil speaking be put away from you, with all malice and be kind, tender-hearted, forgiving one another even as God for Christ's sake as forgiven you."

Jesus said that when two or three are gathered in his name, he will be there among them. Where the spirit of the Lord is, there is the one true church. We are more than three together here, gathered here to worship God in the spirit of love. As we worship God with all our hearts, we are being the church here, now, in community with one another.

Being the church is to be a worshipping community.

Being the church is also being a teaching and learning community, a community of loving minds that seeks the truth of God's beloved world wherever it may be gathered.

The early disciples of Jesus called him "Rabbi." When people gathered around Jesus they came to listen and to learn from him. When Mary met the risen Christ at the empty tomb she called him "Rabbi," which means "teacher." To be the church means to use our minds to discern the truth, the truth about this marvelous world into which we have been born, and to learn the sorry truths of the gods of profit, the gods of war, the gods of vengeance.

Being the church means that we teach God's presence in all the world. Like witnesses in a court of law, the church must tell the truth to what we have seen and what we have experienced in all the sciences, in all of history. All truth is God's truth. To love God with our minds is to love what God loves, and God loves the world.

The Gospel of John begins by pointing to this truth: "In the beginning was the word, and the word was with God and the word was God. All things were created by the word, and without the word nothing was created. What has come into being was in him, in him was life, and the life was the light of all people. And the light shines on in the darkness, and the darkness does not overcome it."

Where the spirit of the Lord is, there is the one true church, apostolic and universal.

Where two or three are gathered together in the spirit of Jesus, there is the worshipping, teaching, learning, witnessing community that is the church.

We, here, now are being the church, at worship, and as witnesses to the love of God.

A Telling Witness

Matthew 17:1–9, Psalm 2

This story of the transfiguration of Jesus appears in three of the four Gospels, in Mark and Luke as well as in Matthew. The story is referred to as well in the Second Letter of Peter in the New Testament. Apparently, the first-century Christians felt this was a really important story. And yet to us, it is a rather fantastic story, don't you think? This story of three disciples having the same religious experience of Jesus's face and clothing being transformed by luminous light, of mysterious figures appearing and then disappearing in a cloud, a story of a voice emanating from the midst of the cloud.

But the same story, with little variation, appears in all three of the synoptic Gospels. According to the Gospels, this is the testimony of men who were there, the testimony of the witnesses to the event. This is what the witnesses said happened!

Can you imagine what a Washington lawyer would do with witnesses who sounded like this? My clinical psychology friends would say, "Visual and auditory hallucinations are not unusual among schizophrenics with a history of religious mania." My social psychologist friends who study religion would say, "Well, 30–50 percent of the people we survey in this country report having religious experiences, but most people don't talk about them for fear people will think they are crazy." I know my college students would say, "Whoa, what were those guys smoking, anyway!"

What does this story mean? It is no wonder it is puzzling to us. It was puzzling to the men who experienced it, Peter, James, and John. When Peter suggests that they build three shelters on the mountaintop, one for Jesus and one for Moses and one for Elijah, Mark's Gospel says Peter was so terrified he didn't know what he was talking about—hardly a flattering comment about the man who is credited with being the founder of the Roman church. But certainly understandable, don't you think? Wouldn't you have been frightened by such an experience?

So, here is a story that was very important to first-century Christians, and perhaps very confusing to folks like us in this century. I'd like to take a few moments to think with you about this text, to try to sort it out with you. I want first of all for us to look at what the text meant to the writers of the New Testament, why it was so important to them. Then, second, I would like us to think about what possible meaning it may have for us today.

I think the first clue to the text's early meaning gets by us almost before we even know it. The text begins, "Six days later Jesus took with him Peter and James and his brother John up a high mountain." Six days later than what?

What has just occurred in the story is that Peter has publicly recognized Jesus as the Messiah, and Jesus has begun to teach his disciples that, as the Messiah, he must suffer and die, and the disciples argue with him about this. Peter even tells him: "God forbid this. This must never happen to you." But Jesus tells Peter: "Get behind me, Satan! You are not thinking about divine matters, you are thinking of earthly matters." Jesus tells Peter anyone who would be his follower must be prepared to lose his life for his sake. Jesus has told his disciples: If you call me the Messiah, then you had better be prepared for the consequences. Those who want to save their life will lose it, and those who lose their life for my sake will find it.

These are not, of course, comforting words. They are words that fly in the face of expectations about a Messiah who is a national savior. It is as if Jesus were telling Peter, If you believe I am the one our people have been waiting for you might well think again, for what I am about is not what most people think the Messiah is about!

So, the stage is now set for our text this morning. The disciples have been challenged to think and rethink just what it may mean to call Jesus the Messiah. It is then, at that time, when disciples are wrestling with what it means to call Jesus the Messiah, that he leads them up the mountain.

Now, why go up a mountain? Why not go to the desert or to the Jordan River? Because in the Hebrew scriptures the high mountains are the place where God comes down to meet his servants. Remember where Moses received the Ten Commandments? Remember where Elijah heard the voice of God? In the mountains, the high place where the earth and the heavens come closest together in that three-story universe, is where God met his servants.

And the cloud? Why the voice out of the cloud? Because in Hebrew tradition the cloud is one of the symbols of the presence of God. Remember, as the Hebrews fled the Egyptian armies through the wilderness, it was a pillar of cloud that led them forward. If you were a Hebrew who knew your tradition you knew you met God in the clouds, high up on the mountain.

And who is it that the disciples meet when they follow Jesus to the place where God's revelations take place? They find Moses, the great founder of the nation, the great giver of the Torah, the holy law. And they find Elijah, the great prophet of the nation, the herald and forerunner of the expected Messiah. Like summer follows spring, so the Hebrews believed, the Messiah will come after Elijah appears.

So, there they all are together, Moses, the authority of the ancient sacred law; Elijah, the embodiment of the prophetic tradition; and their friend, Jesus. And the three are talking together, just like friends do. Then, a bright cloud overshadows them all and they hear a voice from the bright cloud saying: "This is my beloved son. I am well pleased with him. Listen to him. Listen to him. Listen to him."

Well, the meaning of this seems pretty clear. Don't camp out on the mountain with the old legal tradition. Don't settle down on the mountain with the prophets who still await the Messiah. Listen to Jesus! This is my beloved, my chosen! Listen to him!

Here is epiphany, the recognition, the realization, the great aha!, the dramatic disclosure of the authority of Jesus endorsed by the historic spiritual leaders of the nation and confirmed by the very voice of God. And we who went up the mountain, hopeful but doubtful, saw it. We heard it. We believed it. We followed Jesus down the mountain and on to Jerusalem, up that other hill called Calvary. Then beyond that cross, beyond his tomb, we heed his voice and we follow him still.

This is why the New Testament church prized this story. It recounts the disciples' religious experience. It is their witness that Jesus of Nazareth is the Messiah, the intimate of Moses and Elijah, the chosen of God. Listen to him! He is not what you expected. He is more than you expected. Listen to him.

Now, what might this text mean to us, we who do not expect to find God in the clouds and do not gather on Camino Cielo on Sunday mornings because it is the highest point we can reach with our cars? We don't dwell in that three-story universe. We are not a people who await a national savior or expect a prophet to usher in a new messianic age. But in some other respects we are not all that different from those first-century Christians.

Some of us wrestle with just what it means to be a follower of Jesus. I know I still do. I keep wanting Jesus to be the Messiah I want him to be, the Messiah of my childhood, the Jesus who watched over the Methodists in my daddy's North Dakota churches but who really didn't look out for the Lutherans and the Catholics who worshipped in strange ways and drank real wine at communion. But I keep finding that Jesus doesn't love Methodists any more than he loves anybody else. More important, he doesn't love them any less, either. I keep hearing Jesus remind us that God sends rain upon the just and the unjust alike, and that it is not my gift to know the heart of another man or woman, so I ought not judge them. I keep hearing Jesus say it is my responsibility to manage my own heart, my own loves, my own loyalties, and to seek to love what God loves.

Some of us may want Jesus to be a good Congregationalist, a Jesus who would vote the way I do at congregational meetings, and who goes away mad with me when I'm not in the majority at those meetings. But I keep finding Jesus offending not only his antagonists but even his disciples by what he says and what he does. I keep hearing Jesus call me to move beyond my current notions of perfected love. I keep hearing Jesus praying for his enemies. I keep hearing Jesus pray that his disciples will all be one.

Some of us may want Jesus to be a good Democrat or a good Republican, to endorse our vision of a just political order. But I don't hear Jesus saying anything about Democrats or Republicans. I keep hearing him talk about feeding the hungry, clothing the naked, visiting the prisoner, welcoming the stranger, comforting and healing the sick, welcoming the children. I keep hearing Jesus offend the nationalists of his day because they are too exclusive, and offending the internationalist defenders of empire as well because they are not inclusive enough. I keep hearing Jesus calling those whose lives are consumed by private ambitions and parochial interests to offer their lives to the cause of justice and compassion that transcends all political boundaries.

Sometimes I want Jesus to call me to do great things, to set me at his right hand, so I'll be recognized and honored and loved for the super person I am! But I keep hearing Jesus ask: "Are you able to drink the cup that I drink? Can you be faithful even over little things?" I keep hearing Jesus say, Don't let your righteous passions and principles distract you from the actual person in need now by the side of the road, from the woman in the crowd who reaches out in need, from the little children who look to you in innocence with trust and hope.

Be faithful where you are! Who knows what God may bring you to do?

A Telling Witness

ORDINARY TIME

On Having the Time of Your Life

Ecclesiastes 3:1–9, 1 Thessalonians 5:1–11

"Ordinary Time"

There is only one question I need to ask you. "If you are not having the time of your life, who is?" Jesus told his disciples, "I have come that you might have life, and have it abundantly." Are you having the time of your life? If you are not, who is?

It is not a trick question. My experience, and what I read and hear about other people's experience, tells me that many people in our culture find that the time of their lives is being had by someone else, by the social institutions that regulate when we work and when we shop, by cultural expectations about how we are supposed to spend our time, by nagging little voices in our brain that say, "Oh, it's six o'clock. I'm supposed to be having supper," or "Oh, it's ten-thirty. Church is supposed to be over." In these years of COVID precautions, I hear again and again, "I just want to get my life back!" Or that refrain I hear again and again in grocery store lines: "Oh, I would really love to do that. But I just don't have time." And so, I ask, If you don't have the time of your life, who does?

We live in a culture that is dominated by awareness of time. Does anyone here this morning not have a watch or cell phone? Someone has argued that it is the invention of the clock that has altered civilization more than any other invention. Without the ability to precisely measure time, our technological civilization could not be created, much less coordinated. Industrial organization depends upon people working by the hour, for so many hours, to be paid by the hour. The precise measurement of time allows rockets to be launched and satellites to be placed in orbit. Time has become the means for measuring activities, while the activities themselves, what we are actually doing, has become subordinate to the length of time it takes to do it.

A doctor is supposed to spend eight minutes with each patient. A classroom period should be sixty minutes long. "I made it to Los Angeles in ninety minutes!" So? Is your life richer, or more meaningful, more abundant for that?

Time used to be significant because of what human beings were doing. What we did made time significant, planting, cultivating, harvesting, preserving, mending. The scripture from Ecclesiastes reflects this view of time: Time becomes meaningful because of what we do with it. I want to suggest that having the time of our life these days requires us to recover something of this sense of time as understood in the Bible, and as understood by most people throughout history until the Industrial Revolution.

The Greeks had two words for time. "Chronos," from which we get our word chronological; and "Kairos," for which there is no equivalent word in our language. Time is kairotic when what happens then changes ever thereafter the person who experiences it. When a father tells his daughter at the church door on the day of her wedding, "It's time!" he is not telling her it is ten minutes after two p.m. Later, when this daughter, now married and pregnant tells her husband, "It's time!" she is announcing a kairotic moment that will bring a new life into their lives and alter the time of their lives ever after.

If we are to have the time of our life, instead of being had by the institutions of our culture for which time is an abstract measurement, we need to reclaim the meaning of kairotic time in our life.

The seasons of the church year are about kairotic time. They are not chronological seasons. They are seasons that derive their meaning from what you and I and God do during that season.

This means that the seasons of the church year are attuned to the deepest, most basic aspects of our human life. This means that it is the God of all creation whose activity gives these seasons meaning, not the gods of our culture.

Let me say what I mean by this. The gods of our culture, the forces upon which our culture depends for its survival, are the gods of Hollywood, are the networks, the advertising industries, all of whose business it is to convince us our life is not a good enough life, that real life is only possible when the Messiah comes—and the Messiah that will make life meaningful and beautiful wears Calvin Klein jeans, drives a Chrysler sports car, or drinks Moet champagne, and watches the new fall lineup on NBC. The gods of our culture persuade us to yearn for, to lust for, to despair until we own what they are selling, or see what they are producing.

It is then, the gods of our culture tell us, that the Messiah arrives, when life will be beautiful, when we'll all have clear skin and thick, curly, bouncing and behaving hair, and life will be as exciting as a Pepsi-Cola ad—forever! That's when we'll have the time of our lives!

But the God of our Lord Jesus Christ is not a god of our culture, but the God of all time—the God who brings worlds into being and takes worlds out of being—the God whose actions we celebrate in the church year. We call Jesus the Christ, which is the Greek word for the Messiah. Jesus, whose living and dying and rising and living spirit put an end to the illusion that real life is some other life. Jesus, whose life and dying and rising revealed that God is with us in this life, and that there is nothing in life—nothing in life—that separates us from the love of God.

In the church's liturgical seasons there is a time for waiting, and there is a time for making ourselves ready. God is in that time. We call it Advent. There is a time for receiving and there is a time for giving. God is in that time. We call it Christmas and Epiphany. There is a time for introspection and there is a time for acting. God is in that time. We call it Lent. There is a time for suffering and for dying. God is in those times. We call it Holy Week. There is a time for being raised to life again. God is in that time. We call it Easter. There is a time for celebrating this community of new life in which we find the time of our lives rendered meaning-full. God is in that time. We call it Pentecost.

We are now in that season of the church year called Ordinary Time. God is in this time. Ordinary Time is those portions of the church year that are not defined by some special mystery of Christ's birth, life, death, and resurrection. This does not mean that Ordinary Time is "ordinary" in the sense of "nothing special." Rather, it is that time of the church year when we consider the overall meaning of the life and teachings of Jesus.

And what does it mean to call Jesus the Christ? It means that Jesus is the one who puts an end to our messianic longings, to the longing for life to be fundamentally other than what it is. Jesus delivers us from the illusion that life, real life, will begin at some future time. That is why we call him the Christ.

Jesus is the one who confronts us with the truth that the very life we have is God's gift to us, that this is the scene in which God meets us, calls us, and day by day loves us amid our ordinary lives, revealing to us that nothing in life is really ordinary, but that God's grace makes the experience of life itself extraordinary.

Ordinary Time. This is the time of our life. And God's good grace enables us to appropriate each day as a gift most precious.

The seasons of the church year are kairotic seasons, they are seasons that scale the heights and plumb the depths of human meaning. In a culture that worships speed and change, the church year raises the possibility of eternal meaning and timeless truth. Where else will you look, in this culture, for help in having the time of your life?

I want to close with a quotation from that great English poet John Donne who was Dean of Saint Paul's Cathedral in London in the early seventeenth century. It seems to me he says all that needs to be said about the seasons of our life, about Ordinary Time, and about what we need to know to have the time of our life. Here is John Donne:

"God made the Sun and Moon to distinguish seasons, and day, and night, and we cannot have the fruits of the earth but in their seasons: But God hath made no decree to distinguish the season of his mercies. In paradise, the fruits were ripe, the first minute and in heaven it is always Autumn, his mercies are ever in their maturity. We ask panem quotidianum, our daily bread, and God never says you should have come yesterday, he never says you must again tomorrow, but today if you will hear his voice, today he will hear you. If some King of the earth have so large an extent of Dominion, in North, in South, as that he hath Winter and Summer together in his Dominions, so large an extent East and West, as that he hath day and night together in his Dominions, much more hath God mercy and judgment together: He brought light out of darkness, not out of a lesser light: he can bring thy Summer out of Winter, though thou have no Spring: though in the ways of fortune, or understanding, or conscience, you have been benighted till now, wintered and frozen, clouded and eclipsed, damped and benumbed, smothered and stupefied till now, and God comes to thee, not as in the dawning of the day, not as a bud of the Spring, but as the Sun at noon to illustrate* all shadows, as the sheaves in harvest, to fill all penuries,** all occasions invite his mercies, and all times are his seasons."

Thanks be to God.
Amen.

*illumine, fill with light
** poverty, great need

Religion 101: G-O-D

Romans 8:31–39; Philippians 2:1–13

When I was teaching religion classes to college students, there tended to be three groups of students in my classes. There were students who had been brought up in church and Sunday schools who were eager to have their existing ideas about God and Jesus confirmed. They were often disappointed with my class.

There was a second group that had been raised in church and Sunday school who had rejected it all. "I don't believe God created the world in six days. I don't believe that stuff about Noah and the ark or Jonah and the whale. I do not believe God ordered the Israelites to kill all the men and boys in the Canaanite cities they invaded. I don't believe Mary was a virgin or that God was Jesus's father. I don't believe any of it, and I don't want to waste my time and money with this class."

I told them that I didn't believe in the same God they didn't believe in, so not to worry about it. Just read and come to class.

The third group had had no upbringing in the church and their ideas about God and Christianity were based largely on what they heard at the mall at Christmas or heard from TV evangelists as they surfed the TV channels looking for "Seinfeld" or "Friends." This was by far the more interesting group of students and in some ways the easiest to engage. They were more prepared to think about God and religion with open minds.

For example, if I read the scripture from Philippians, "Have this mind among you that you have in Christ Jesus, that although he was in the form of God did not count equality with God a thing to be grasped, but emptied himself, taking the form of a servant," the first group of believer-students would say, "Yeah, right on!" The second group would say, "Yeah, yeah, Jesus was God, but I don't believe it, and even if he was, so what?"

The third group might actually listen and learn that in the first century, when Paul lived, there were people who claimed to be God, or in the form of God, literal divinities or demigods, the offspring of the mating of gods with humans. Students were interested that the Roman emperor Caesar Augustus was worshipped as the "son of God and the savior of the world" within his empire.

What distinguished Jesus of Nazareth in the first century is not that some people came to regard him as a divine being—but rather that, unlike Caesar, Jesus did not claim to be God or to be God's equal. He did not claim divinity, but humbled himself, gave his life not as a military conqueror but as a teacher who did justice, who loved kindness, who walked humbly with God, as the prophet Micah would have put it.

The point is, I'd tell students, you don't live in the first century. You know you don't live in a three-story universe—a flat earth floating on waters beneath the earth, under a glass dome with stars and planets fixed in the glass dome. You know you don't live in a world composed of just four elements—earth, air, fire, and water. And you know what? You don't have to believe in a god that made sense in a three-story universe when you know you live today in an expanding universe, on a small planet in a huge galaxy, which is just one of billions of galaxies in the universe.

What kind of God worthy of the name would want you to live your spiritual life in the first century, but the rest of your life in the twenty-first? Once the students heard that—once they got that—religion class began to be interesting.

This morning I would like us to think together for a few moments about what it is we mean when we speak of *God* in the twenty-first century. Is there a shared reality, a consensus of meaning we point to with that word?

And what do we mean when we speak of the love of God? I propose that we begin in a very general way, a somewhat abstract way, to speak of "God" and the "love of God."

Then I want us to think about the apostle Paul's experience of God and the love of God as he wrote about them in the scriptures read this morning.

Finally, I want us to think about what it means to believe in and to experience the presence and love of God in our own lives.

What do I mean when I say the word "God"? I mean this: God is the mysterious power that brings all things into being and sets limits to the being of all things. God is that reality that when you cease to believe in him doesn't go away (a paraphrase of Peter Videbeck). After all, a God whose reality depends upon my believing in him, or your believing in her, could hardly be the source of all being. If that were the case, the reality of God would depend on me, rather than my being depending on the reality of God.

I don't know about you, but I am clear that I am not the mysterious power that brings all things into being! I have a hard time even writing a sermon!

And the "love" of God? What might we mean by that? Well, I think we must speak of the love of God in both a general sense and a personal sense.

We see the love of God in the general sense in that we all showed up this morning. I don't mean that we showed up in church. I mean that we showed up at all! I didn't make that happen, and neither did you. The love of God, in the general sense, is that the earth turned toward the sun once more this morning. I didn't make that happen and neither did you!

The love of God, in the general sense, is that the biochemistry of the organisms of the earth and sea and sky are working today, are still working today, despite what you and I are doing to the planet. That is the love of God, the grace of God, in the general sense.

That there is something instead of nothing, that in this expanding universe we are. That is the love of God in the general sense. And our being at all is amazing, beautiful, mysterious, wonderful, and bountiful.

Turning now to the apostle Paul, although the first-century consensus about the nature of the earth and the nature of the cosmos was much different than it is in ours, Paul's idea of God and the love of God can be understood in our own world today.

Paul did not buy the idea that Caesar was God or that any political power or human institution was the source of all being. Paul did not have a sentimental notion of God, a God who spares the earth all danger and disaster. The God Paul wrote about was a God known amid calamity, disaster, and death.

We should remember that Paul had been thrown into prison many times, flogged nearly to death. Five times he had been punished with thirty-nine lashes, three times beaten with rods, stoned once, shipwrecked three times, adrift on the sea for a night and day before being rescued. On his travels he was in danger from bandits, in danger from his own people as well as from Roman political authorities. Thirsty, hungry, cold, naked, and all the while anxious about what was happening to the people he loved in the churches he helped to found (1 Cor. 11:21–28). It sounds a lot like what goes on in our society and among the nations of the world today.

And in this kind of society like our society, Paul wrote, "Neither height, nor depth, nor persecution, nor nakedness, nor peril, nor swords, nor political rulers or pagan demigods, neither life nor death, nor anything in the whole created order can separate us from the love of God in Christ Jesus." Paul chose these words purposefully, carefully, because he had experienced all these things in the world.

So, what did Paul mean when he said G-O-D? Clearly, he did

not mean some Tinkerbell deity who grants every wish or some superhero divinity who intervenes to clear a path through all of life's obstacles and evils. Oh no!

God, for Paul, is the God of Jesus who was beaten, scourged, crucified, dead, buried. Only such a God could matter to the poor, beaten, oppressed, people of the Roman Empire. A God who was with them even in and through their suffering, a God from whom not even death itself could separate them. This was God whose reality and whose love brought all things into being and whose love continues beyond the end of all being. That is what Paul experienced, and that is what he preached and wrote about.

So now we have thought about God and the love of God in a general sense, and about how Paul thought and wrote about God and the love of God in his own life.

But what about the love of God in the personal sense in our own lives? After all, that is what interests most of us, most of all, most of the time. What about me, God? How do I know that you love me? How do I know that I matter to you?

Well, how does this strike you? The mysterious power of the universe that brings all things into being and sets limits to all beings, that God, the God of the planets, the God of the expanding universe, has brought you into being. Just how much more personal significance do you need than that? I mean, really!

Each one of us—we are each a one-off! There will never be, in all evolutionary time, another you. The love of God in general becomes the love of a personal God when we claim our personal existence as the unlikely gift of grace, which it surely is, in the stream of evolutionary time!

The love of God in the specific, personal sense is experienced when we can say "God, I thank you for my existence. I thank you that I am!"

But that is not the end of it. The love of God, in the specific, personal sense goes on from there:

> "I thank You God for most this amazing day:
> for the leaping greenly spirits of trees
> and a blue true dream of sky; and for everything
> which is natural which is infinite which is yes
> (i who have died am alive again today,
> and this is the sun's birthday; this is the birth
> day of life and love and wings: and of the gay great
>   happening illimitably earth)
> how should tasting touching hearing seeing breathing
> any—lifted from the no of all nothing—
> human merely being doubt unimaginable You?
> (now the ears of my ears awake and now the eyes of my
>   eyes are opened.)"

(Thank you, E. E. Cummings!)

The mysterious power that brings all things into being becomes a personal God when we acknowledge that we are a person, a person who resonates with the freedom of our being in this beautiful world, limited though we may be.

Then it is we are able to say, to pray:

I thank you, God, for this amazing day.

Amen

Good News for Parents

Exodus 20:1–17

"You shall not kill. You shall not steal. You shall not lie. You shall honor your father and your mother."

One might wonder why there is a need for a commandment that parents be honored. Killing, stealing, lying—these are clearly serious offenses, and the reasons for their prohibition are not hard to discern. But they make rather grim company for the fifth commandment, especially since honoring one's parents might seem a sentiment hardly in need of enforcement. Yet, there it is, squarely in the middle of the Decalogue. "You shall honor your father and your mother, that your days may be long in the land that the Lord your God gives you."

Since in the weeks ahead, the Florists Transworld Delivery service will nourish the admonition to honor mother and father and, yes, even grandparents, for motives quite other than those which were Moses's, it might be beneficial to reflect upon the significance of our religious tradition in order to keep a balanced perspective.

It is important to note, in the first place, that the fifth commandment follows those commandments that are intended to establish the sanctity, holiness, and utter authority of God. You shall have no other gods…You shall make no images of God…You shall not take the name of God lightly…You shall not dishonor the day set apart for the worship of God. And you shall honor your father and your mother. The first five commandments deal with the principal authorities in human life — God and parents. Indeed, parents do occupy a position in the lives of their children that is almost godlike. It is one of the things that makes being a parent so awesome. And Freud, of course, regarded God as our childhood's experience of parental power, dimly recalled and projected upon a mysterious universe.

Can you recall what it was like to be a child looking up an adult? Shoes as big as your whole body. A belt buckle as big as your face. A pair of hairy nostrils over which peer huge eyes. In a split-second, arms can reach down and snatch you five body lengths distant from the floor to a tabletop. The strength of parents cannot be resisted. Their anger can turn your body rigid. Their soothing voice and touch can lull you to blissful sleep.

Freud rightly discerned the powerful influence of parental authority in shaping children's fears and fantasies. But he missed the significance of his own Jewish heritage's insistence that the power and authority of God are holy, and that which is due to God must not be confused with that which is due to parents. Both God and parents are powerful authorities throughout our lives. But God is holy, the unnamable, wholly other. Parents are creatures, instruments of creation, deserving of honor but not to be confused with the final authority, the final power, which is God's alone.

This is a distinction that Jesus reportedly understood at an early age. When he was a young adolescent on his first trip to Jerusalem his parents lost track of him. When, after three days of searching, they found him in the temple debating with the elders he rebuked their anxiety with a question: Why are you looking for me? Did you not know that I would be in my father's house? It is a distinction he carried into his adult years when he taught his disciples that being his follower might mean having to sever relationships with their mothers and their fathers if those relationships challenged the authority of God in their lives.

Parents are instruments of creation and the bearers of love in our lives, and they are to be honored. But they are not God and are not to be confused with God, obeyed as if their word expressed the absolute holiness of God.

This is one of the great applications of the good news of Jesus Christ. He proclaims liberty to the captives—to those children whose parents try to assume the power of God in their lives, parents who demand unquestioning obedience, parents for whom children are property, extensions of their own egos, their own powers in the world. The Gospel proclaims the priority of God in the life of the child. The honor due parents comes after the commandment, "You shall have no other gods before me."

This is good news for children, but it is good news for parents as well. For if children honor their parents as parents instead of obeying them as gods, then parents, once again, have a chance to be people, to be humans, to be creatures, to be themselves. The past ninety years have been rather hard for parents in our society. They have suffered under a misunderstanding fostered by some branches of psychology that implied that parents were to blame for every hare-brained thing their children did wrong. Nor have children been slow to exploit the power this distorted view of human relations has fostered. As the streetwise delinquent in *West Side Story* explains in "Gee, Officer Krupke": "Our mothers all are junkies, our fathers all are drunks; golly Moses, naturally we're punks!"

I taught courses in child development for many years. One of the painful things through the years was the appearance in class of a super-mother, one who had read every book on child psychology she could get her hands on, had found out that most of them disagreed with each other about a number of things, and was immobilized with the fear that if she frowns at her two-year-old when he throws his oatmeal on the cat the child will develop a complex and join the Hell's Angels when he is seventeen.

Such parents know, rightly, that they are important authorities in their children's lives. But in their anxiety over this awesome responsibility, they lose sight of the other forces at work in the life of their child, or they confine the child anxiously within their own orbit rather than trust the child to influences beyond their control. But parents are not expected to be gods in their children's lives. Indeed, they had better not try to be. What they can be is fallible. What they can have are needs of their own. What they need not be is as consistent as a computer. And what the child will know is what it means to be loved by a human being, which is not really such a bad thing to learn as a child!

Honor your father and your mother. Negatively, it means not to confuse parents with God in your life. Positively, it means to accept them as they are—human beings, frail creatures whom God loves no less than God loves little children. And when parents get to be sixty or seventy years old, they have not ceased to be God's children. That they did not have total wisdom when they raised us, that they did not always know exactly what to tell us, what to let us do, and what to prevent us from doing, does not mean that they did not love us and intend to do well by us. Perhaps the greatest honor we can do our parents is to let them down off the pedestal of our imaginations, where we are inclined either to idolize them or to flog them as gods who failed (as indeed they must fail), and to accept them as people—people who need forgiveness as well as respect, who need honest relationships with their children perhaps more than with anyone else.

But this is difficult. I do not think we honor anyone by being dishonest, and there is no relationship in life more filled with ambivalence than the relationships between parents and children. These conflicting, contradictory feelings are hard to acknowledge to ourselves, hard to acknowledge to them. Perhaps that is why we are commanded to honor them.

Parents are those persons who give us life and the means to live it, and who set limits to our living it. "Have a piece of cake… but only one piece." "Here is a new dress for you, be careful not to get it dirty."

"I want you to make your own decisions. Your mother and I will be terribly disappointed if you don't do well." "Always be honest with others, but don't hurt their feelings."

Parents are those persons from whom we want to be free and independent, and to whom we want to be able to return when independence becomes terrifying. Parents are those persons we do not want to tell us how to live our lives, especially when we are living with them. And they are often the first persons we want to talk to when we have problems about what to do in life.

We have mixed feelings about our parents, most of us. Honoring our parents means being honest about those feelings, honest about them to ourselves so that we can enter forgiving, accepting, loving, grateful relationships with our parents.

There is something of this ambivalence in Jesus's relationship with his mother. Of course, she worried about him, wanted to know what he was about on his travels. Of course, she would try to see him when his ministry brought him near to Nazareth. She was probably perplexed by his passion to preach, which seemingly showed greater concern for the larger family of Israel than for his own family at home.

But Jesus used the analogy of the closest human ties he knew to express the urgency of his message of the kingdom, the analogies of relations between parents and children, father and son, a father's great love, a sibling's jealousy. When he found persons who rationalized their neglect of their parents by saying there were more important religious causes to support, he showered them with scorn. We do not honor God by dishonoring our parents, even as we are clear to acknowledge who is the Creator and who is the creature. And so, at his death, Jesus showed his concern for the welfare of his mother. He required John now to take responsibility for her care.

The ambivalence—the mixture of feelings that is the stuff of parent-child relationships—these take a lifetime of living to understand, to realize, to accept. It is grace that opens us to honesty in the honor we show.

We do not know when we are young what it is like to grow old. The commandment to honor our fathers and our mothers, to treat them honestly, with acceptance, with forgiveness, can keep us attuned to the truth of our own mortality, to the truth that we, too, are aging children who one day, if we keep the commandment, may have children who will honor us with honesty, forgiveness, and acceptance.

A Geography of Love

Song of Solomon 7:1–8:4; 1 John 4:7–12

The first thing I was taught in seminary about interpreting a biblical text is to find out what it meant at the time it was written, what it meant to those people, at that time, in that culture. Then the next question the preacher needs to ask is, what does it mean now, to us, in our culture, at this time?

We already know that when we begin to talk about love, it's complicated. And if we are going to talk about romantic love, well, it's especially complicated. The whole idea of romantic love has been a source of conflict in the thinking of the church since the first century. So, I am going to spend a few minutes this morning talking about the cultural and historical situation for the scriptural texts used in this morning's service, to try to clarify what those texts meant in the first century, to those people. Then I will have a few things to say about what I think is the Gospel for us in those texts. What is the good news about love, even romantic love, on Valentine's Day 2016?

The first texts we read this morning were the Call to Awareness: "In the beginning was the word and the word was with God and the word was God. All things were created through him and without him was not anything made that was made…and the word became flesh and dwelt among us, and we beheld his glory full of grace and truth."

In Greek the word that gets translated as "word" in English is "Logos," and Logos in the first-century Greek culture meant a great deal more than does the word "word" in English. For the Greek culture, the Logos was the cosmic pattern and the cosmic purpose actively expressing itself in the world. In modern biology we would say the Logos is like the DNA of the world, the biological code that determines the physical form of every living being.

In addition, the Greeks believed this eternal creative Logos was reasonable, which meant human beings could understand it because the Logos created us human beings to be reasoning creatures. These Greeks would say that the reason that mathematics that works on earth works in outer space as well is because it is all the creation of the rational, organizing, creating Logos.

So, when John begins his Gospel saying the rational, creating principle, pattern, and power of life became flesh and dwelt among us he is saying two revolutionary things to the men and women of that culture. The first is that Jesus shows us the rational pattern, the determining principle, and purpose of life in a form we can understand. And the second revolutionary thing is that this rational pattern, principle, and purpose of life is made known in the flesh, "the word became flesh and dwelt among us, and we beheld his glory."

This statement challenged the prevailing belief in Greek culture that it was the flesh, the body, that prevented men and women from knowing the fullness of life. For the Stoic philosophers, it was the flesh, the body, that prevented humans from the full knowledge of God.

But the central teaching of Christianity is the incarnation, the message that God is revealed in the physical body of Jesus, and that God's love is to be expressed and conveyed in the human, mortal flesh of beings like you and me.

The message of the Gospel is that God loves us, creatures who relate to the world through our senses. This being the case, how did the human body, and especially human sexuality, get such a bad reputation in the history of the church?

Holy Saint Valentine's Day, what went wrong?

To teach that God is incarnated in a human body also flew in the face of what was considered science in the centuries in which Christian theology was first developed.

Aristotle had taught that the world and all that is in it is made up of four elements—earth, water, wind, and fire—and that these four elements are controlled by two competing powers, levity and gravity. Gravity draws the heavy elements of earth and water down to the ground. Levity pulls the spiritual elements of wind and fire upward, and all motion is the result of the struggle among these conflicting elements as they seek their ultimate destiny.

Our physical body of earth and water struggles against our spiritual body—our souls, which seek to escape the body, to rise, rise, rise to the heavenly realm, where there will be no more struggle, no more change, only peace, endless peace, eternal peace with God.

If this is the accepted understanding of how the world works, then it follows that it is our bodies that keep us from knowing peace with God. This is why our bodies must be tamed, must be subdued, why our desires must be denied if we are to be at one with God.

When we understand that this is the historical context of the early church's theology, then the church's history of denigrating the body and the flesh, especially sexuality, can be understood. It is why the church for centuries taught that sex is only good if its purpose is to procreate.

The poetry from the Song of Solomon had its origins hundreds of years before the Christian era. Any man or woman who has been blessed to know romantic love recognizes the meaning of the poetry. The woman's navel is not an allegorical baptismal font, nor is the heap of wheat that is her belly an allegorical reference to the bread of the Lord's supper. The poem is about a beautiful woman in the amplitude that was regarded as beautiful in that culture. Twiggy women were not the beauties of that age.

But the early church for centuries insisted that the poetry of the Song of Solomon must be understood as a metaphor of Christ's love for his church. Never mind that the poetry predates Jesus's birth by many centuries. The poetry *must not* really be about human love! Astonishing, I know!

As human beings it is through our senses, through our bodies, that we experience the world and come to know the world. We are blessed with reasoning minds, yes. But the data, the information about which we reason comes to us through our senses. Without our bodies we would not be, not be at all. We are sentient, bodied beings. If we are to be Christians, then we must be sensuous Christians. What other option is there?

E. E. Cummings has help for us who hope to be a sensuous Christian.

> i thank You God for most this amazing day:
> for the leaping greenly spirits of trees
> and a blue true dream of sky; and for everything which
>   is natural which is infinite which is yes
> (i who have died am alive again today,
> and this is the sun's birthday; this is the birth day
>   of life and of love and wings: and of the gay great
>   happening illimitably earth)
> how should tasting touching hearing seeing breathing
>   any-lifted from the no of all nothing- human merely
>   being doubt unimaginable You?
> (now the ears of my ears awake and
> now the eyes of my eyes are opened)

That is a long explanation of the context for this morning's texts. Let's spend a few moments thinking about what they mean for our lives today.

One way the Christian life has been characterized is that it is a pilgrimage. Life is a pilgrimage…"climbin' up the mountain children…. we didn't come here for to stay." And a pilgrimage is, by definition, a long journey that is taken with a purpose in mind, with a chosen destination. The pilgrimage of the Christian life can take years and years, cover all kinds of terrain, some smooth and easy, some rocky, difficult, some swampy, even hazardous, some requiring great courage.

And what is the purpose of this pilgrimage? What are we to be doing on the pilgrimage of life? As I understand it, the purpose of life is to love. Love is a verb, an active verb with multiple objects and many other pilgrims along our way. And some of these other pilgrims attract our attention!

Here is another poem by E. E. Cummings about a kind of love we may find on the pilgrimage:

> since feeling is first
> who pays any attention
> to the syntax of things
> will never wholly kiss you;
>
> wholly to be a fool
> while Spring is in the world
>
> my blood approves,
> and kisses are a better fate
> than wisdom
> lady i swear by all flowers. Don't cry
> —the best gesture of my brain is less than
> your eyelids' flutter which says
>
> we are for each other: then
> laugh, leaning back in my arms
> for life's not a paragraph,
>
> And death i think is no parenthesis

This poem is one of my favorite poems about romantic love. But romance is but one station in the geography of love. I would like to push that adjective "first" back to the very beginning of a child's life.

"Since feeling is first" is the truth about a newborn child. The baby has no sense of an adult's syntax of things. The baby knows no syntax other than its own feelings. A baby does have feelings and it's the mother's and father's task to ignore the syntax of things in their lives and to attend, to intuit, to interpret the language of the infant's feelings. It is the parents who are illiterate so far as the infant is concerned, and if its feelings are not attended to its own brain will not develop. Infants who are only diapered and fed and left to themselves do not thrive. Their brains do not develop as they should. They develop a condition called marasmus.

Attentive love is not merely an option for a human infant. Attentive love is a developmental necessity. It is far from romantic. Caregivers must pay attention to the syntax of the child, must learn to read its face, its body language, the sounds it makes. The infant's responses to its mother's face, its father's face, its caregivers' faces and voices are its own language.

After about a year a child begins to figure out that these people around her just don't get it, and so she begins to make the sounds these people make, and parents exclaim, "*She's talking!*" And life becomes easier for the child and for the parents—at least for a few years.

Life's pilgrimage begins in love, requires love, and without that attentive love at its very beginning all human pilgrimages will never begin. The basic human phenomenon is not the individual. The basic human phenomenon is a relationship, a relationship characterized by love. The rational, creative, engendering Logos of God becomes known to us by our seeing, our hearing, our tasting, our touching, our feeling. Our bodies are not the real problem.

Our problem is whether we use our bodies for loving purposes or for selfish purposes, for acts of kindness and compassion and justice, or in ultimately futile attempts to assert our own individuality, and to guarantee our own security and immortality.

As Saint Augustine observed, "You have made us for yourself, O God, and our souls are restless until they find their rest in thee."

A Sermon for Earth Day

April 22, 1990

Psalm 19

First United Church of Christ, Northfield, Minnesota

This Sunday we celebrate Earth Day. It is rather ironic that the only persons in the country who don't already know this are people who live away from the sound of radios and TVs, who never see newspapers and magazines. People who live so close to the earth that its celebration is more likely a daily experience. These folks may not know it is Earth Day, but perhaps they are people who least need to know it.

We have used prayers and images from several Native American traditions in our worship this morning because they disclose a reverence for the source of all life. They speak eloquently of our place within the natural world. In Chief Seattle's words: "The earth does not belong to us. We belong to the earth. We did not weave the web of life: we are merely strands within it."

There is much within Native American spiritual traditions that should sound familiar to us. Humble awareness of our place within the created world is a key element within our own Judeo-Christian tradition. We find it in the writings of the prophets. We find it in the Psalms. Insightful though they are, we need not look to the great souls of the New World like Chief Seattle to be informed about our proper place within creation. There are great souls in our tradition who have articulated a similar vision.

Take for example Saint Francis of Assisi, whose great hymn "All Creatures of our God and King," we sing repeatedly each year in this congregation. Francis would have well understood our Native American brothers' and sisters' prayers and songs, for he was inspired by the same spirit as moved them. Saint Francis would be a good patron saint for Earth Day.

But Saint Francis hasn't seemed to attract much notice among those who celebrate Earth Day. This is too bad because he is really a spiritual ally in their cause. Francis was the kind of young man in the thirteenth century who had no interest in his wealthy father's cloth business. He didn't see the value in being wealthy; it wasn't the kind of upward mobility that appealed to him. Birds—they had a kind of upward mobility that fascinated him, and clouds, and the stretch of trees, and the reach of mountains.

This privileged child of a wealthy merchant looked at the role models of his family and said: "No thank you. Where you are leading, I do not care to go."

Francis seems to have been one of those persons who understood the psalm I read this morning. For him, the heavens did speak of the glories of God. For him, the firmament, the earth with its grasses, its flowers, its trees, its birds, and animals did speak of a creative power at work around him. Not that they had a voice, of course, not that they uttered words.

Nonetheless, they were eloquent! The colors of flowers shouted. The trees danced. The hills rose and flowed down again like the limbs of a peacefully slumbering woman. Somehow, despite his city upbringing, Francis knew that whatever power made the flowers also made him, that whatever power sustained life in the smallest of birds, was sustaining his life as well. His famous hymn expresses his sense of kinship with the natural order of the world.

What, I wonder, would Saint Francis think about the state of the earth today? Where would he find "flowing water pure and clear, making music for his Lord to hear?" What might he have thought about those who have built upon his father's mercantile motivations, his father who had him disinherited because he used his money to build a church rather than build the business? What would Francis think, standing above the smog-clouded cities of the twentieth century, listening to the pollution warnings that are given with the weather report?

Well, he probably would not have known what we mean by "nature," any more than a fish knows what water is. But it is Francis's lack of alienation from what we call nature that makes him so fascinating and so instructive a figure for us today. You see, one of the great predicaments we face as human beings on Earth Day 1990 is how to overcome our own alienation from what we call "nature."

But I must not use the word "overcome" because the word "overcome" itself expresses what is at the root of that alienation. We presume there is something that we must do, something we can do that will somehow let us slip back into some mythical grove out of which we have wandered, allow us to clamber our way back onto some previous perch from which we have fallen. Our alienation is expressed in the presumption that there is something we can do to restore a lost order of things when it is, rather, our presumptuous attitudes and doing that are the cause of the disorder, the alienation.

This is not, of course, a new insight. It's as old as the third chapter of Genesis. Wordsworth, in prophetic lamentation, put it this way in the nineteenth century:

> "The world is too much with us; late and soon,
> Getting and spending, we lay waste our powers;
> Little we see in Nature that is ours.
> We have given our hearts away, a sordid boon!"

When we look at the catalog of ecological blunders we have committed in this century we may wish there were some pristine Eden to which we could return, some untainted splinter group of the human race we could join so, like creatures in the rest of the animal kingdom, we could just follow our noses from our birth to the grave.

But of course, we cannot because we are the beings who, although a part of the natural order of things, have an odd way of sticking out in the order, stepping out of the procession of instinct-led creatures to reflect on from where we have come and to where we might be going—and whether it might not be more comfortable to get there by car.

Reinhold Niebuhr used to say that we are the kind of creatures who exist at the juncture of nature and spirit. When we deny our spirit, our lives sink into sentimental romanticism, and we deny we have control or responsibility for our actions. "You know, it's our hormones, we just do what comes naturally." Or, more horrible, we conjure images of some innate, racial superiority and rationalize our brutality toward whomever does not look like us as the inevitable outcome of a perverse notion of natural selection.

On the other hand, when we forget, or deny, that we ourselves are a part of nature, we perpetuate the illusion that we have capacities, abilities, wisdom, and knowledge that allow us to escape the consequences of our actions, that we can destroy our web and still not fall out of it. "Don't worry! It's perfectly safe!! Would we be allowed to sell it if we didn't know what its consequences were?"

We are creatures, bodied beings, a part of nature. But we are also spiritual beings, creatures who anticipate a future, who look at a rock and see therein a statue: who look at a statue and are reminded of sacrifice, and struggle, and of ideas like truth and beauty and freedom.

The psalmist knew what Niebuhr meant. After exclaiming, in wonder, at the glories of the earth and heaven—the natural world—he turns his attention to the highest spiritual achievement of his culture, his religion. He marvels at the teaching of his religion:

the law of the Lord, perfect reviving the soul, rejoicing the heart, enlightening the eyes.

But then comes that startling phrase about the purpose of his religion's teaching: "Moreover, by them is thy servant warned. But who can discern his errors? Clear thou me from hidden faults. Keep back thy servant from presumptuous sins: let them not have dominion over me!"

What is the meaning of this "presumptuous sin"?

According to my dictionary, to presume something is to take something for granted, without having proof to the contrary. I presumed, for example, that you would gather here at ten thirty today for worship. I didn't know for sure that you would be here, but I acted as if you would be here not having proof to the contrary. Being able to presume things, to act regarding an unknown but anticipated future is a human spiritual capacity, something like faith, actually.

I am presumptuous, on the other hand, if I presume too much, if I engage myself in activities for which I have no authority or permission. Then my action is arrogant, even offensive. I may presume, for example, that you will be here at ten thirty Sunday morning. But if I preach for sixty minutes and still expect you to be here, I am presumptuous, certainly arrogant, and possibly offensive, presuming that you all have nothing better to do than listen to me go on and on.

Presumptuous sins, which the psalmist prayed to be delivered from, are those actions we undertake not knowing the consequences, that are unwarranted, given the state of our knowledge, that are arrogant, even offensive. Presumptuous sin is behavior that presumes too much because we know too little, or because we have an inflated sense of our own power and importance.

Further, in the psalmist's understanding, the consequences of such activities boomerang, come back to haunt us, or in his words come to "have dominion over us."

Think if you will of the draining of the wetlands of the Minnesota River valley. This was activity our fathers and grandfathers presumed was OK. After all, those wetlands could be put to better use raising corn. Or so they thought. But acting where they did not know and not being able to foresee the consequences of their actions, the nesting areas of birds were destroyed, and the natural predators of insects disappeared. The natural filtering system of plant-filled ponds was destroyed, and polluted waters made their way over open ground, eroding the land as they flowed.

The loss of slowly released pond water into the drainage basin meant the decline of the feeder streams into the river and the loss of fish and the loss of forms of wildlife that depend on water for movement, food, and protection. Now the counties of western Minnesota seek state funds and foundation grants to try to reclaim the wetlands to reverse the consequences of presumptuous acts.

"Thou flowing water pure and clear, make music for thy Lord to hear."

What do you think, Saint Francis?

"Keep back thy servant from presumptuous sins: let them not have dominion over me."

Think of the slash-and-burn techniques that are destroying tens of thousands of acres of tropical forests to plant crops that will bring cash to the owner for a few years. The birds, whose songs we enjoy in Minnesota, are losing their winter nesting sites. The animals whose habitat is these forests are losing their homes. Native plants, the earth's pharmacopoeia, are bulldozed to oblivion before we even know their names or their contribution to our ecosystem. The planet Earth that depends on the trees in these forests to consume carbon dioxide and to release oxygen warms and warms. Rainfall patterns across the face of the globe are altered. Human populations are forced to migrate, victims of prolonged climatic changes and drought. All this to raise cash crops that in a few short years exhaust the soil and leave nothing of value in their place.

What do you think, Saint Francis?

"Keep back thy servant from presumptuous sins: let them not have dominion over me."

In his book *The End of Nature*, William McKibben points out that the very idea of a natural world, an order of life and being outside the influence of human mind and hand, has become extinct. The greenhouse effect, global warming brought about by what we have propelled into the skies, means that nature—the interactive biological context within which we have evolved—has been dramatically altered.

McKibben is not hopeful about more human doings being able to extricate us from the dominion of our presumptuous sins. "Deep ecology," he says, "suggests that instead of just giving better orders we learn to give fewer and fewer orders—to sink back into the natural world. The problem is that nature, those independent forces that have surrounded us from our earliest days, cannot coexist with our numbers and with our habits."

Well, Saint Francis, how do you like them apples?

"Without Alar, thank you. They are beautiful the way they grow."

We may listen to Saint Francis or to Chief Seattle. We may listen to Isaiah's vision of the peaceable kingdom where we and the rest of the animal kingdom live in peace together. We may listen to the ecstatic words of John's Revelation on the isle of Patmos, his vision of a beautiful city, resplendent amid clear-flowing streams and sparkling sunlight. Or we may listen to the psalmist.

In every case, however, the message is the same: "The earth is the Lord's and the fullness thereof, the world and all that dwell therein." To know this and to order our lives in harmony with this is the way of salvation.

There is a story told about Martin Luther. An anxious believer asked him, "Father Martin, if you knew the world were to end tomorrow, what would you do?" Luther replied. "If I knew the world were to end tomorrow, I would still plant my apple trees."

That is a response appropriate for our lives on Earth Day 1990—a response appropriate to our knowledge, in harmony with our present needs, and full of faith in the regenerating power of the God who placed our ancestors, as well as us, in a garden, and bade us care for it.

Reflections on Psalm 23

Have any of you ever spent time with sheep? On my grandparents' homestead in North Dakota, they raised horses and cows and chickens and turkeys and pigs—and sheep. The sheep were brought into the pen by the barn at night to keep them safe from coyotes, who prowled and howled out on the prairies. When my cousin and I got old enough to do chores, feeding the sheep in the morning was one of the jobs we had. In the morning, we boys would carry five-gallon pails of feed to dump into the twelve-foot-long feed troughs for the sheep.

The sheep were never patient to get their food and would crowd around us. One time a sheep came up behind me as I was dumping a bucket of feed into the trough, put his head between my legs, and jerked his head upward. He sent me on my first solo flight, up and over the feed trough, ker-splat on the ground.

I learned that sheep, like people, are not all alike, and I had a different kind of respect for sheep after that. I came to take a more personal interest in Psalm 23, which I had memorized in Vacation Bible School.

In the psalmist's world, it would have been the gods of the Canaanites or the Philistines who claimed to be the Lord of life. In Jesus's day, it was Caesar Augustus who claimed to be the son of God, the prince of peace, the ruler of the world. In the Gospel of John, Jesus warns about false shepherds, those who are leaders who care for the sheep only because they are paid to do so, not because they know and love and truly care about the sheep.

In our day, when we pass through the mall or watch the ads on television, we are bombarded with the message: "You need this. You must have this. You must wear this. You must look this way. You are not good enough; you are not acceptable unless you do what I tell you. Follow my lead! I'll lead you to the bottled water, and Oregon green sweatpants—and restore my own profit line."

I love the quiet, meditative beginning, "The Lord is my shepherd." But in a society and a culture that bends itself to persuade us to heed other voices and to trust in them, it might be well to read Psalm 23 a bit more assertively: "NO. The Lord is my shepherd. He makes me lie down in green pastures. He leads me beside the still waters. He restores my soul."

"He leads me in paths of righteousness for his name's sake." There is that word, "righteousness," which seems like a strange word to come out of the mouth of a sheep. But righteousness in Hebrew means living in the right relationship with the whole created world around you. If you are a sheep, don't try to live like a donkey. If you are a human being, don't pretend to be God. If you are a human being, "Do justice, love kindness, walk humbly." That is what it means to walk the path of righteousness in the name of God.

In the next verses of Psalm 23, the psalmist changes from talking about God in the third person. He begins to talk directly to God. It is no longer "He makes me lie down," "He leads me." It is now you, God, who is with me, you who is my companion in life's dark valleys, it is you, God, who comforts me, it is you, God, who set a feast before me, even in the presence of my enemies. It is you who anoints my head with healing oil, and it is you who fills my cup to overflowing.

It is as if the psalmist realizes that the leading, caring, guiding God he has been thinking about is not a shepherd directing his sheep from a distance. Rather, he experiences God as immediately present in his life, in that very moment, as close to him as the breath of his own life. He moves in his psalm from ideas about God to conversation with the God who is the companion of his life.

And he finishes his psalm with this astonishing realization: "Surely, goodness and mercy shall follow me all the days of my life, and I will dwell in the House of the Lord, forever." That is an epiphany. That is a revelation. That is the realization of his ultimate destiny.

I once heard a preacher say that Shirley, Goodness, and Mercy are the names of the three sheep dogs that belong to the good shepherd. If you are fond of big, friendly, faithful dogs you can enjoy that image, if you wish.

Or you might simply rejoice in astonished wonder that although we are as simple sheep, we are, nonetheless, the beloved lambs of God.

"You have made us for yourself, Oh God, and our souls are restless until they find their rest in you." —Saint Augustine

The Personal God

Romans 8:31–39; Philippians 2:1–13

The mysterious power that brings all things into being becomes a personal God when we acknowledge that we are persons, persons who resonate with the freedom of our being, limited though that freedom may be.

Perhaps we can sense the marvel of it all if we remember that at its Latin root the word "person" means a mask through which an actor speaks his or her part on stage. As a "persona," we are one of the masks of God through whom God is acting upon the stage of the earth.

Some of us are bad actors, and we refuse our lines, we miss our cues, or we insist on writing ourselves into the hero's role, a role in which we dominate the stage rather than play within the ensemble of a most extraordinary cast of people, plants, animals, lights, and props. When the stage is commanded by bad actors the play is a tragedy.

For some of us, a service of worship helps us recall our place in the drama of life, helps us remember our lines and to hit our marks. For some people, however, church doesn't do that. For them, something else does.

The love of God in a specific, personal sense is experienced when we are able to say: "God, I thank you for my existence. I thank you that I am!" But that is not the end of it. The love of God, in the specific, personal sense goes on from there:

> I thank You God for most this amazing
> day: for the leaping greenly spirits of trees
> and a blue true dream of sky; and for everything
> which is natural which is infinite which is yes
> (i who have died am alive again today,
> and this is the sun's birthday; this is the birth
> day of life and love and wings: and of the gay
> great happening illimitably earth)
> how should tasting touching hearing seeing
> breathing any—lifted from the no
> of all nothing—human merely being
> doubt unimaginable You?
> now the ears of my ears awake
> and now the eyes of my eyes are opened
>
> (Thank you, E. E. Cummings!)

For some of us, the natural world communicates the mysterious reality and love of God and reminds us of our place within the natural order of the earth. For other people, the natural world speaks no words, offers no prompts about their role in the life of the world.

For some of us the eyes of our eyes are opened by the innocence of a child's trust in the goodness of the universe. For some, kids are just an annoyance.

For others, the ears of our ears are awakened to God's extravagant love by beautiful music. Music can and does heal our wounded spirits, does transport us to the truth that is healing, and restores a harmonious spirit in the midst of a discordent world. We have been blessed in these past years to have such musicians make such music in our midst.

For others, the love of God is made personal in the words of another person, a friend who reminds us that we share our lives together and that love without an object is like a dammed-up stream—it has nowhere to flow, nowhere to go, and we stagnate, because we are made to love.

Sometimes that friend is a writer, and I close with the words of such a friend:

> "Life will break you. Nobody can protect you from that, and living alone won't either, for solitude will also break you with its yearning. You have to love. You have to feel it. It is the reason you are here on earth. You are here to risk your heart. You are here to be swallowed up. And when it happens that you are broken, or betrayed, or left, or hurt, or death brushes near, let yourself sit by an apple tree and listen to the apples falling all around you in heaps, wasting their sweetness. Tell yourself that you tasted as many as you could."
>
> —Louise Erdrich, *The Painted Drum*, p. 274

So it is, we work out our own salvation with fear and trembling, for it is God who is at work—before us—within us—beyond us—enabling us to be, and to will, and to work for God's good pleasure (Phil. 2:12,13).

Amen.

A COLLEGE
OF THE CHURCH

Homily for the Opening of the Academic Year 1995-96

August 31, 1995

"When Jesus saw the crowds he went up the hill. There he took his seat, and when his disciples had gathered round him he began to teach them." (Matthew 5:1)

These words are Matthew's entrée to that collection of Jesus's teachings that we have come to call the Sermon on the Mount. These collected teachings in the fifth, sixth, and seventh chapters of Matthew's Gospel were remembered and prized by the early church not only for their remarkable insight and power but also as evidence of Jesus's prowess as a teacher. Matthew closes his record of these teachings with this observation, "The people were astounded at his teaching, for, unlike their own teachers, he taught them as one having authority" (Matt. 7:28-29).

Teaching is not listed among the miracles attributed to Jesus in the Gospels. However, I find it quite astonishing, when I take the time to think about it, that the means chosen by Jesus to do his work in the world were those of a teacher. It may be that because we stand so close to the activity of teaching that we do not fully appreciate what a strange and marvelous, even mysterious activity it is.

But consider this, if you will. According to my Introductory Psychology text, it is the movement of air from my diaphragm that causes my vocal cords to vibrate, vibrations that when shaped by my tongue, soft palate, and lips form waves of alternating amplitude and frequency that travel through this room and strike your eardrums. The vibrations of your eardrums are transferred via three tiny bones to the cochlea of the inner ear where these physical vibrations cause tiny hair cells to vibrate, which tickles the auditory nerve, initiating electrical signals along the nerve, which travels to the thalamus and thence to the auditory cortex of the brain.

There, depending on how the electrochemical activity of my brain initiated this whole process, and how the electrochemical processes of your brain decode its neural stimulation, you may either laugh or cry, rejoice or despair, repent and renew, be impelled to anger, or propelled in curiosity to the library, or to yawn, or to any of the practically innumerable other responses that we are accustomed to seeing on the faces of our students in our labs and classrooms.

Such are the physical and neural mechanics of oral teaching, which do not begin to address how our minds instantly assess semantic subtleties—irony, metaphor, paradox, inference, exaggeration, or understatement for effect. What arises in the electrochemical bath of our brains becomes intellectually stimulating, emotionally moving, spiritually powerful, motivating, perhaps even life-directing, and transforming. Such are the vicissitudes and powers of the spoken word. Such are the perils and possibilities for teachers as we enter our classrooms, studios, and laboratories.

How will those ideas and feelings and hopes and possibilities that arise in us move through the space between us and our students, and be reformed within their minds, bearing the potential to alter the direction of their lives and thereby the lives of all whom they meet?

Teaching may not be a miracle, but it is surely one of the wonders of human being.

When my dad retired from the pastoral ministry, he gave me a little plaque he used to keep on his desk. It says, "God so loved the world that he didn't send a committee." Those of us who have labored past the dinner hour in committees on this campus will have a particular appreciation for that sentiment. I have even heard some of my more conservative colleagues suggest that committee meetings have infernal rather than divine origin.

Although that plaque expresses a kind of grim truth about committee work, some of the time it is theologically inappropriate, especially in a college of the Lutheran tradition. Luther taught that all honest work can be done as vocation, as answer to the call of God. So I would suggest, at the beginning of this academic year, that while God so loved the world that he did not send a committee, God did send a teacher among us in Jesus, and calls us likewise to be teachers, to be not merely a committee, but a faculty, committed to witness to truth as it emerges in our understanding, to strive for justice in our smaller and larger communities, to express and celebrate beauty in the arts, and to invite our students to heed their own calling as scholars and servants in a needy world.

Let us pray.

O thou who did send your son into our midst as servant and teacher, grant us hearts grateful for the opportunity to teach. Grant us the grace of open hearts and minds that as persons devoted to the whole of truth we may graciously learn from one another, willingly share our common burdens, and truly rejoice in our colleagues' success. Grant us courage to challenge error about us and humility to acknowledge it within ourselves. So may we be women and men obedient to the call to teach, in the spirit of Christ we pray, amen.

Members One of Another

Romans 12:1–12

CHAPEL ADDRESS, NOVEMBER 14, 1991

I hope that we might think together this morning about our life together as a college of the church. Paul's letter to the congregation at Rome is as much a context for what I hope we will think about as it is a specific text for the morning. For, among other things, Paul's letter addresses two basic human needs that must be taken seriously in an educational institution: the need we each feel to be included within some human community; and, at the same time, the need we each have to feel some sense of significance as an individual.

These two needs, to feel included and to feel like a person in our own right, are part of our experience throughout our whole life. We see these needs in the two-year-old child who loudly cries "Look at me! Look at me!" wanting to be noticed, wanting to stand out. But he cries it to Mommy and Daddy, his most important human community, without whose support and pleasure he feels bereft and alone.

We see these needs in the twelve-year-old who protests to his parents—"I'm twelve years old. I'm big enough to go away to camp"—and when at camp, cries himself to sleep because he is homesick and misses his parents.

We see these needs in the twenty-two-year-old who faces graduation from college with pride and optimism because of what she has achieved during four years of college. But she also feels a devastating sense of loss as she leaves the friends and the community she has become a part of during those four years, and she feels a daunting anxiety about establishing her life in a new city, in a new job, alone.

We see the action of these twin needs—to be a part, that is to be a member, and to be apart, that is to feel independent—throughout the whole lifespan.

Parents experience this with their grown children: "I want you to be independent, to be out on your own, to think for yourself. But I don't want you to be so independent that you move that far away from home, that you join that political party!" I want my children to live apart from me, but I still want them to be a part of my life.

You students experience this shift acutely when you go home after a semester at college. You have become accustomed to being independent, to being apart from your family. You are not the young man or woman who left that home three months before, and there is often an awkward rearranging of expectations and behavior that goes on with your parents and your friends at home.

As faculty we experience it as the need to achieve in our profession, to have our work published, and our teaching praised. We want to stand out in our profession, and so we devote hours to getting our work noticed and praised. But at the same time, we don't want to stick out too far from the compact consensus of our colleagues, for we, too, can be devastated by loneliness. We long for an evening of human companionship in which there is no need to work, to compete, no need to shine. We would trade the next publication for someone to be there, to share coffee with us when we return from the office late at night.

We watch our aging parents struggle with the same two needs, to remain independent and to feel included, not forgotten, but loved, still a part of their children's lives.

It is parents' task to understand and to engage in this lifelong dance with their children. From an undifferentiated existence in its mother's womb, the child becomes a person apart from its mother but in the same moment becomes a part of its family. In our society, if all goes well, the child moves apart from the family to become a part of the playgroup, and then a part of the school. But it is still a part of the family, although the part it plays in the family changes—indeed must change as that child's particular gifts, particular graces become evident and distinctive in the world.

In our society a child will usually move apart from the birth family altogether, to become a part of a new family, to experience being a partner in other relationships, perhaps a marriage, perhaps a career, perhaps both. As these movements take place, as we respond to these two needs in ourselves and in those close to us, we are changed, and all with whom we have been in relationship must change in response. Good parents recognize these needs and alter their own lives to enable the increasing independence of their children.

When Paul wrote, "We are members one of another," he was thinking theologically, but he was also describing this profound truth about human development. Parents are constituted parents by virtue of the child in their midst just as much as the child is constituted the child by virtue of the actions of the parents. There is a dynamic mutuality in this relationship between parents and children that nurtures the need to feel a part, a member of the family, and apart, an independent person with gifts and a life of its own.

This is how it is. We are members one of another, in a changing, human community, from womb to the tomb, from cradle to the grave.

"But what," you may well ask, "does this have to do with our life here? What does this have to do with Saint Olaf College?"

What it must do was first suggested to me twenty years ago in an essay by John Seeley. Seeley points out that insofar as a college takes its educational task seriously, it does so in continuity with the purpose of all good parenting, to be a community that stimulates and nurtures the development of the persons within it. Which is to say, in so far as it takes its educational task seriously the college stands in loco parentis, it stands in the place of parents, not to perpetuate the environment and rules of the home, but to create a context that enables a student to move apart from the smaller community of the family in order to become a part of a larger community of persons, a larger community of ideas, a community with, perhaps, a larger vision of life's meaning and purpose and possibilities.

In loco parentis has become a discredited notion in higher education. But look more closely. In loco parentis does not mean "crazy like your parents!" In loco parentis has become a dirty word in higher education precisely to the degree that colleges mirror our society's low regard for the high calling of parenthood, precisely to the degree that colleges have rejected their task of nurturing the emerging gifts of young men and women in an ever more complex and diverse human community. What other institution in society can perform that task?

When the college acts properly in loco parentis it enables a student to understand herself as having become the very person she is, because she is a member of her particular family, yes, but also because of her and her family's relationship to the institutions of school, and of government, of commerce, of religion, of the arts. The college's task, in loco parentis, is to enable students to move beyond their immediate family intellectually, emotionally, and spiritually, to move toward an understanding of themselves as persons whose intellectual relationships reach back to the very beginning of recorded history.

It is the college's task, in loco parentis, to help students understand that they are biochemical and psychological selves whose roots stretch back through evolutionary history. It is the college's task, in loco parentis, to help students know that they are spiritual selves who are informed by this past, but who reach forward in imagination to communities not yet formed but which they will form, in part, by what they learn here, in part by virtue of the choices they make here and the relationships they establish here.

We are members one of another, and insofar as we, the college, take our educational task seriously, we are a community in loco parentis. We constitute a community called the college, to enable the emergence of the individual gifts among us.

But this much could be said about any college that sees the task of teaching to be the further development of the person within a complex community of persons. What, if anything, has this to do particularly with being a college of the church?

As a college of the church, the relationship that defines the limit and possibility of our life together is not our relationship to the Modern Language Association, or the American Chemical Association, or the American Psychological Association, or any professional association, important as these relationships may be to our individual lives and to our disciplines.

As a college of the church, the relationship that defines the limit and the possibilities of your life as students is not the corridor on which you live, or the major you study, or the Young Republicans, or the Young Democrats, or OLGA, or the Student Congregation, important as these relationships may be in your lives as students. As a college of the church, we know that these are penultimate relationships; serious, but secondary. They define important possibilities for our lives, but they are not, finally, the definitive relationship in which we know ourselves to live and move and have our being. We are a part of them, yes. But in a fundamental sense we are apart from them as well.

Insofar as we know ourselves to be a college of the church, we know our possibility and our limit is established in our relationship to the gracious one whom Jesus called, Abba, Father, the one who calls this world into being. This puts in context and into perspective all other relationships of which we are a part.

Insofar as we know ourselves to be a college of the church, we know our possibility and our limit is established in our relationship to the righteous one who weighs all human institutions in the scales of justice—disclosing the limitations of institutions, the partiality of all versions of political correctness. This ought to free us from defense of the status quo and turn our minds and hearts in hope to fuller realizations of the reign of God in our midst.

Insofar as we know ourselves to be a college of the church, we know we are not called simply to transmit the culture. Any good college or university can do that. Rather, as a college of the church, we are called to teach in faith and hope the possibility of culture transformed by the vision of a community in which there is no distinction between male and female, slave and free, Jew and Greek, nation and nation. Therefore, insofar as we are a college of the church, our first concern ought not to be politically correct but to be theologically responsive.

As a college of the church, we are called to be a part of that community in which, so far as grace permits, each person's gifts are characterized by sober judgment, by generosity, humility, mercy, cheerfulness, patience, forgiveness, prayer, and joy.

"So, we, though many, are one body in Christ, and individually members one of another. Having gifts that differ according to the grace given to us, let us use them."

Seeley, John, "The University as Slaughterhouse," in *The Great Ideas Today, 1969*. Chicago: Encyclopedia Britannica, 1969.

Getting to Know Me

Luke 9:18–20

SAINT OLAF CHAPEL, OCTOBER 15, 1981

There are times when it feels like the fabric of our life is coming unraveled. I am referring to those instances—sometimes fleeting, sometimes of longer duration—when the sense of who we are in the world, that sense of confidence in the integrity of our own identity, begins to fall apart.

You may recall having had an experience something like this. You are newly arrived on campus, a freshman, bringing with you the accomplishments of four years in high school—a letter winner in two sports, a member of the school choir, recognized as an excellent student by your teachers. At home, when students saw you, they called you by name, they knew what your accomplishments were. The teachers knew you, too, and would give you a hopeful look when the rest of the class was stuck for an answer, hopeful for a reason, because you usually could come up with some answer to their questions. What you had done and what you could do were well known to you and to those around you.

But here you are new on campus. Those accomplishments of the last four years are unknown to anyone here except yourself. The roles you played in school activities, the positions you held in the youth group back home, the familiar routines of home that channeled your energies and brought you recognition in the town, at church, at school, are all wiped away in this new setting.

It is not that you have amnesia. But it is as if everyone else has amnesia so far as you are concerned. You have no history in their lives. You have no identity, so far as they are concerned.

And for a moment, or for a week, or for a month, you struggle with the alternate terror of having no one know you, no confirmation of your identity, and with self-condemnation for feeling so foolish and childish. And you may struggle with the loneliness that is a part of such a crisis of identity.

The failure of our social group to acknowledge us as persons with a history, with gifts that are valued and useful, can trouble us for weeks and months.

Did you know that faculty members can experience this too? Faculty experience this not only when we are new on campus. Faculty members experience this confusion at professional meetings where, unknown and unrecognized, we wander hotel lobbies with ill-disguised unease, uncomfortable, scanning the crowd for a familiar face that will recognize us, uprooted as we are from the comforting routines of the office and the classroom.

No, adolescents and youth are not the sole possessors of identity confusion and loneliness. These are part of the human condition, and they continue with us throughout the course of our lives.

We should note that the cause of such identity confusion is not always the collective amnesia of our immediate group. Sometimes the cause is a change in our ability to function physically. If we are accustomed to being physically active and then find ourselves disabled, all those ways in which we expressed ourselves physically, all those roles we filled through physical activity are suddenly denied us. Our accustomed sources of self-esteem are gone.

Then, questions such as "What use am I? What good can I do? What's the point of it all?" haunt our daydreams.

The occasion for these feelings may be an accident, a broken leg or arm. Or it might be illness. Does anyone remember what it is like to recover from mono? But the cause may also be our failing strength as we grow older, the flagging of our energies so that we cannot work as long or as hard as we once could.

It may be the awareness that our hearing is not as good as it once was or that our memory is not as quick as it was. It may strike us as funny when a young person holds a door open for us and then not as funny when, later, trying to open the door ourselves, we find ourselves grateful that he did.

Illness, accident, aging itself can challenge our sense of identity. The crisis of midlife, the failing of confidence in old age, all can raise frightening questions about our worth, about our purpose, our identity.

In the scripture read this morning, Jesus asks his disciples, "Who do men say that I am?" And then follows this with, "Who do you say that I am?" The usual focus in the scripture is upon Peter's answer, "You are the Christ," rather than on the fact that Jesus raised the question.

But I notice that as Luke records the incident, Jesus is surrounded by his disciples but is alone in his activity of praying. That is, he is with his hand-picked comrades, but in the deeper sense of their participating with him in his life, they are not with him at all.

"Who do men say that I am?" "Who do you say that I am, my friends?"

Not idle questions at all, but questions born out of the need to locate oneself within a social group and to hear from other people that who one feels oneself to be is known, is acknowledged, is valued. It seems to me that there is much to be gained from an analysis of these experiences, these challenges to the integrity of our sense of identity.

One thing we see is that our lives are always lived in the context of some historical, social group and must make sense within that context. If Peter had answered Jesus's question "I think you would make a great president," it would have been an incomprehensible answer in that society, as incomprehensible as if your career counselor told you, "I think you have a great future as the keeper of camel herds in Dundas."

No, our identity must make sense within the context of the needs and opportunities and expectations of our time and culture. Further, we see that we are not really self-sufficient beings. We require the physical support of others, as well as the emotional support and love of other human beings from the first moments of our life onward. In time we come to exchange the close physical expressions of affection we received as children from our parents for more distant, socially approved forms of social acknowledgment and approval: a smile in greeting, a warm handshake, a word of appreciation.

But we still need that attention, that interaction, that appreciation. When it doesn't happen in our lives, we suffer. We need the support of other human beings.

The problem is, of course, that our social groups change. We move from one community to another, or our closest friends leave us, or sickness or death overtakes them. That is why an identity that is founded on the reflection of our being in the eyes and words of others is so vulnerable, subject to such devastating experiences of crisis. Social groups do change. Nonetheless, the social, cultural setting of our lives contributes an important dimension to our identity as men and women. It is the scene within which we act out our lives.

Another thing we may notice about our sense of identity is that it is built upon specific talents, abilities, skills that we have developed in the course of our life. If I wish I were someone else, I don't become someone else just because I move to a new town. The "I" that moves to a new town is still the same person who plays tennis somewhat, and plays cello less than that, who knows some things about psychology and religion and almost nothing about mathematics.

Whatever the social setting, I know more about the Methodist Church than anyone wants to hear. None of those things I can do and know change simply because I live on campus instead of home. Granted, what I know and can do may be more useful in one setting than in another, but my skills, such as they are, and my knowledge, such as it is, are portable.

Now, the good news about this is that the gifts you have can be cultivated, the knowledge you currently have can be expanded, skills that you don't have, you can acquire. In short, you aren't stuck with the identity components you brought with you to college. In fact, if we all aren't much more interesting, complex, multitalented people after spending four years together we have been exchanging money and services under false pretenses.

There is another dimension to identity that I haven't found adequately addressed in the psychologies I have studied. It has to do with whom it is in the privacy of our internal dialogues we allow to pronounce the final word about the value and the purpose of our being, those things that are at the core of our identity.

There is no shortage of persons, no shortage of agencies, willing to pronounce that word about our lives. Turn on your television: Does the Oil of Olay lady pronounce the final word about the value of your physical being? Pick up your textbook. Does Freud pronounce the final word about the source and destiny of your life? Does Skinner? Open your PO box: Does the registrar pronounce the final word about your intellectual being? Open your newspaper: Does Wall Street pronounce the final word about your worth, about your destiny?

Unless you are one of those fortunate children who grew up in Lake Wobegon, where all children are above average, you have grown up in a society that picks you over, rates you, grades you regarding your physical attractiveness, your physical agility and strength, your intellectual quickness, your emotional stability, and the frequency which you shower and use your toothbrush.

And not seeing anyone with a red cape and a big letter "S" emblazoned on their chest in this room, I know that from time to time a part of your internal dialogue has been, "I am not really a super person." "I am not as smart as 'x.'" "I am not as good a singer as 'y.'" "'A' plays tennis better than I do." "I don't have the ethical sensitivity and commitment of 'z.'" "My graduate record exam scores place me in the 80th percentile. Where did I go wrong?"

Getting to Know Me

But who is it that pronounces the final word, the Authoritative Word about your life, the word before which all other judgments about your identity are made relative?

Is it the army that will make a man out of you?

Is it *Cosmopolitan* that will define your being as a woman?

Identity and the resolution of identity crises are, at base, religious problems, which finally can only have a religious answer. Who is the authority before whom I live out the time of my life, employ the gifts of my being within whatever community I may live?

I wish to share two poems with you in closing. The first is a portion of the 139th Psalm. The second is a poem that the Lutheran pastor and theologian Dietrich Bonhoeffer wrote in his prison cell, awaiting execution at the hands of the Nazis in 1945.

> Psalm 139
> O Lord, thou hast searched me and known me.
> Thou knowest when I sit down and when I rise up;
> thou discernest my thoughts from a far.
> Thou searchest out my path and my lying down,
> and art acquainted with all my ways.
> Even before a word is on my tongue,
> Lo, O Lord, thou knowest it altogether.
> Thou dost beset me behind and before,
> and layest thy hand upon me.
> Such knowledge is too wonderful for me:
> it is high, I cannot attain it.
> Whither shall I fly from thy spirit?
> Or whither shall I flee from thy presence?
> If I ascend into heaven, thou art there!
> If I make my bed in Sheol, thou art there.
> If I take the winds of the morning
> and dwell in the uttermost parts of the sea,
> Even there thy hand shall lead me,
> and thy right hand shall hold me.

If I say, "Let only darkness cover me
and the light about me be night,"
Even the darkness is not dark to thee,
the night is as bright as the day;
for darkness is as light with thee.
For thou didst form my inward parts,
Thou didst knit me together
in my mother's womb
I praise thee for thou art fearful and wonderful.
Wonderful are thy works.

Now hear these words from Dietrich Bonhoeffer. (April 3, 1943)

Who am I? They often tell me I stepped from my cell's confinement,
Calmly, cheerfully, firmly.
Like a squire from his country-house.
Who am I? They often tell me I used to speak to my Warder,
Freely and friendly and clearly.
As though it were mine to command.
Who am I? They also tell me I bore the days of misfortune,
Equably, smilingly, proudly.
Like one accustomed to win.
Am I then really all that which other men tell of?
Or am I only what I myself know of my self?
Restless and longing and sick, like a bird in a cage.
Struggling for breath, as though hands were compressing my throat.
Yearning for colors, for flowers, for the voices of birds,
Thirsting for words of kindness, for neighborliness,
Tossing in expectation of great events,
Powerlessly trembling for friends at an infinite distance,
Weary and empty at praying, at thinking, at making,

Faint, and ready to say farewell to it all?
Who am I? This or the other?
Am I one person today and tomorrow another?
Am I both at once? A hypocrite before others,
And before myself a contemptibly woebegone weakling?
Or is something within me still like a beaten army,
Fleeing in disorder from a victory already achieved?
Who am I? They mock me, these lonely questions of mine.
Whoever I am, thou knowest, God, I am thine.

Hearing Voices

Saint Olaf Chapel Meditation, February 9, 1989

I once heard the American philosopher and novelist William Gass talk about watching his son leave his house one morning. Gass said his boy came out onto the front steps of their house and began to narrate his own actions, something like this: "Here he is this Thursday morning. Young Gass is looking trim and ready to ride. He strides to his bicycle. He checks the tires with his thumb, now the front, now the rear. And now he's on his bike, he's on his way, he's down the driveway, he's going, going, gone!"

Professor Gass told us he realized for the first time that he had witnessed a part of his son's internal dialogue, that his adolescent son's life was being lived as if he were being watched and reported on by Howard Cosell or Frank Gifford, or some other sports announcer.

This was a distressing realization for Professor Gass. He whose soul was fed by the subtle nuances of a fine English sentence and the logical precision of a philosophical argument. He whose own internal dialogue resonated with the richly connotative voice of poetry realized his son's internal dialogue seemed to consist of Toyota commercials and sound bites from Sports News Central.

Like witnesses in a court of law, the participants in our internal dialogue can reveal some discomfiting truths about us. As my dad used to tell me—his being one of those voices I hear often in my own internal dialogue—"What gets your attention, gets you."

Our society's economy turns on the ability of merchants to get our attention, to take control of our internal dialogues, and, ultimately, to get us to act in accord with what we hear them saying. Our internal dialogue bears witness to what has our attention, what is occupying that most extraordinary instrument in all creation—our minds.

At times it is embarrassing to recognize whose voice it is we are hearing in our internal dialogue. I am haunted by the Pepsi-Cola jingle that I must have heard when I was about six years old. I know it has been with me that long because it ends, "Twice as much for a nickel too, Pepsi-Cola is the drink for you." The current Pepsi generation needs at least fifty cents, right?

I venture to guess that most of us would be reluctant to be recognized if one or another of the internal dialogues we conduct would suddenly become audible to those around us. And yet Jesus taught us that the first great commandment is to love God with all our heart, and strength, and mind—even in our internal dialogue. There is a discipline for Lent!

There is another aspect to our internal dialogue that is of particular importance to us in an academic community like Saint Olaf. That aspect is our need to come to terms with just who it is that we are living our lives before, who it is that we sense is witnessing the action of our lives. For it is a fundamental truth about our lives that we live always with the sense of being a part of some community in which we are variously being ignored, or recognized, exploited, or honored, noticed, or passed by.

Despite our immediate sense that we are individuals set apart and isolated in our being from all other persons, we are, nonetheless, from childhood to old age woven into a vast fabric of social connections, connections that establish us as persons with identities, value, significance, purpose, and meaning. I am Max and Dorothy's son; Amy, Laurie, and Todd's father; Kathiann's husband; George and Bobbi's friend; a teacher at Saint Olaf; a member of a professional guild of scholars; and a member of the church.

Not only is our internal dialogue made up of many participants but within this vast fabric of relationships we call our life we find ourselves desiring to be singled out, to have our existence witnessed.

It begins very early: "Momma, Daddy, look at me, look at me! Watch me, Momma! Watch me."

That may have changed after a while to "Why is she always watching me?" But until then, it is "Billy, choose me! Choose me!" "Teacher! Teacher! I know, I know!" hand waving frantically in the air.

And then it is: "Oh, I hope she noticed me. I hope she invites me to the party." Or "Oooog! I hope he didn't see me. I don't want to dance with him!"

Then it is "I hope the prof likes this paper: I hope she says something good about my work for once." And still later: "I've sent the article off for publication. I hope it is accepted." And then it is, "I wonder what the reviewers will say?"

Do you see how it works? Throughout our lives we play variations on the theme of *"Notice me!"* and *"Why did I stick my neck out?"* Our internal dialogue reflects both our need to stand out, to be noticed, to be recognized, and our vulnerability when we do stand out. Then our need for safety, for acceptance, for belonging, for being a part of the community can come to the fore.

What William Gass noticed in his son that morning was, after all, not such unusual behavior for a human being, especially an adolescent in our culture. What was unusual is that what is usually an internal dialogue had been overheard.

There is yet another aspect to this phenomenon of internal dialogue and our social existence. It is the truth that as we grow old we pay attention to different participants in our internal dialogue than we did when we were younger. Professor Gass need not have worried that his son would forever imagine himself as the star of *Monday Night Football*. As we grow, our sense of the scope and complexity of our human community grows too. As we grow, we invite new people to participate in our internal dialogue and move the voices that used to gain our full attention toward the back row, almost out of earshot.

Do you remember that girl or guy in the seventh grade who you thought was the neatest thing since sliced bread? Neither do I. But that is just the point. As we mature, we discover we have greater choice about whom we invite to share our internal dialogue. We select certain voices from among the many communities of which we are a part, certain persons that we take as our soul's intimates. When we think, when we speak, when we act, it is with some awareness that we think, speak, and act as participants in this community and not some other, that it is the voices of this tradition and not some other whose judgments we heed, whose counsel we seek, and in whose presence we wish to be numbered and honored.

Martin Luther King Jr. lived within a community of voices that screamed for his death, that denied him the freedom and dignity of a citizen in his own land. But he was free in a way few of us are. Before he had a dream, he had a dialogue. He heard the voices of Harriet Tubman, of Sojourner Truth, of Mohandas Gandhi. He communed with Isaiah and with Amos. His soul intimate was Jesus the Christ. Among the many communities, national and international, of which he was a part, he chose to know himself as a citizen of the Kingdom of God. He chose to heed the voices in his internal dialogue that called him to a life of love and sacrifice for the sake of justice.

These years at college may be thought of as a time during which you may invite different persons and different voices into your internal dialogue. It is a time to consider the difference between "America, love it or leave it," and "Would that I could love my country and love justice too." Mr. Falwell, meet Monsieur Camus.

It is a time to invite into your internal dialogue voices that speak of God's continuing creation, in nature, in history, in personal life. Won't you sit down Mr. Whitehead, there between Monsieur Chardin and Professor Niebuhr.

It is a time to listen to what Mozart heard in the universe as well as what Mr. Brubeck hears. It is a time to hear the voices that have been the spiritual intimates of those who are a part of those communities called humanities, social science, fine arts, natural science.

It is a time to imagine that you are an usher showing an author, or artist, or musician to a seat in the theater where your internal dialogue will take place for the next sixty years. Their book is their ticket for entrance, and there is a whole library full of tickets. Here, Hannah Arndt, won't you take this place? And Mr. Mill, and Mr. James, and Mr. Dewey, you should be comfortable together. And Mr. Faulkner and Ms. O'Conner, how wonderful of you to join me. Father Martin and Professor Erasmus, what an unexpected pleasure. Would you like to sit beside Bishop Augustine? And have you met our friend Dr. Rosemary Reuther?

As men and women, we live, always, within a vast human community. But as men and women, we also choose which voices we will heed within those communities. The voices we heed in the community whose causes we choose to advance by our participation in them may be insistent and enduring, may be just, or may be dehumanizing.

The author of the letter to the Hebrews understood this. That is why he, at first, recites the deeds of women and men, famous and nameless, who had been steadfast in their hope for the promised Kingdom of God. Then, says the writer, "Since we are surrounded by so great a cloud of witnesses, let us run with perseverance the race that is set before us, looking to Jesus, the pioneer and perfecter of our faith."

At the beginning of Lent we may wish to recall the voices that Jesus heard, and those he chose to heed, the voices of temptation, the voices of family, voices of enthusiastic followers, voices of those in need, the voices of denial and derision, voices that sought to entrap and betray him. Rich and complex were his internal dialogues. But it was the voices of the prophets of his tradition and of the Psalms, the hymns of his people, that came to his lips in his time of trial and testing.

At the beginning of this semester, embedded as we are in complex communities of history and scholarship, surrounded as we are with so great a cloud of witnesses, with their causes and hopes, I invite you to listen to the voices of this community, with its history, with its scholarship and with its hope, that we may run the race that is set before us together with those who have gone before, that we may be perfected in the service of the one God whose nature and whose name is Love.

Know Thyself

Psalm 139

SAINT OLAF CHAPEL ADDRESS, OCTOBER 12, 1987

There are two intellectual traditions that inform our life in a college such as this. One is the tradition of the Greeks that teaches that the proper study of man is man, that the unexamined life is not worth living. It stresses analysis of phenomena into their constituent parts and the proper relationship among those various parts. Its motto might be that taken from the Oracle at Delphi, "Know thyself."

The second source of our intellectual life together is the Hebraic, or Judeo-Christian tradition. It stresses the truth that a person becomes a self by virtue of his or her relationship to others. To be is to be a member of a family, a tribe, a people, a nation. To be a person is to be in a community of persons. Its motto would not be "Know thyself" but might be stated, "Know that you are known—and therein know yourself."

There is a kind of tension between these two points of view that is important for our understanding of ourselves as persons, and important for our understanding of our life together as a college. It is a tension that underlies the discussion in our country these past years regarding the relationship of individuals and community. This tension manifests itself in our midst as the uneasy, often-repeated concern expressed from this pulpit for the classmate who gets left behind, left out, ignored, shut out, or shunned in our hectic scramble for individual achievement. Somehow, we sense a betrayal of something basic within ourselves if the excellence we achieve must come at the expense of our neighbor. Must achievement of my most personal ambitions inevitably put me at odds with my colleagues, my classmates, my community?

Were it simply a matter of knowing ourselves as individuals who possess different degrees of intelligence, will, and emotion, the attempt to know oneself would have a kind of clean, cold, analytic edge to it. But that other aspect, the sense that we are known, brings with it an anxious introspection, a concern not merely for right knowing but for right doing as well. "Search me, oh God, and know my heart," the psalmist says, "and see if there be any wicked, hurtful way in me."

Why should it be so hard to know oneself? What is there about self-knowledge that prompted Freud to say, "To be completely honest with oneself is the very best effort a human being can make."

So, to know yourself is to know yourself in your inward dimension. But the self has a life in outward extension as well. Each of us becomes a self by virtue of our participation in a community of selves.

I am the self I am because of the kind of relationships I had and still have. How can I know myself unless I come to a more profound understanding of those relationships and of the factors that helped define those relationships? How can I know myself except as I know the social and intellectual forces that helped shape my mother and father, for it is they who constituted me a particular American boy in a Midwestern Methodist parsonage? To know myself is to know I am a participant in an expanding web of relationships that includes my siblings, my relatives, my schools—a web that extends finally across the globe, backward in time and forward in anticipated meaning, to the edge of my grave—and beyond in imagination and longings of faith.

To know yourself is to know you are a social being. Such knowledge, as H. Richard Niebuhr delighted to remind us, is knowledge that makes us responsible.

Higher education must enable the progressive discovery of that specific self that you are, how the people who surrounded you from the first moments of your life intended you to live and taught you a language and a way of perceiving the world that makes you the specific person you are. To know yourself is to learn the stories, the economic stories, the political stories, the religious stories, and the histories that were told to you so you would have a way of thinking about yourself and your world. To know yourself is to learn how your stories—those that constitute you as the very person you are—differ from and have consequences for peoples in other parts of the world. Those people know themselves through different stories, whose communities, whose cultures, whose histories, hopes and fears are, in part, consequences of our relationship with them.

Knowing yourself is not an exercise for a short-answer test. It is knowledge that makes us responsible. That is why we need to know and are afraid of knowing. If we know, we must change our stories, we must rethink who we are as selves, relearn our histories in a more inclusive light, and reestablish the meaning of our selves within every community in which we participate.

I am thrilled to learn that Saint Olaf affirms in its new mission statement that the self we are committed to know here is the self that exists as respondent in a global network of persons whose passions, hopes, needs, and possibilities are bound up with our own, related to our own. This is higher education that integrates the Greek and Hebraic concern that we know our self.

Part of the difficulty lies in the fact that if we know ourselves, we may have to change ourselves, change our ways of acting in some fundamental way. The 139th Psalm read this morning suggests that this might be the case.

The psalm is a soliloquy, the meditation of a person who is grasped by the mystery of being a person, a person who knows that there is no knowledge he has of himself that surpasses the knowledge God already has of him. Finally, ultimately, at the end of the day, the one who knows the self is not oneself, but God, the one from whom we come, to whom we return, and in and by whom we are.

That is either a comforting or a terrifying thought, to be known bone and sinew, thought and feeling, impulse and act. To sense that our most interior, private thoughts, lusts, fantasies, dreams, aspirations, fears are known, that there is no corner of the room into which we can step to avoid the cosmic camera's eye, no coded language, no cipher, no gesture whose meaning only you know.

Seems hardly fair, doesn't it? No wonder Job, in the extremity of his pain, rails at God, "thou watcher of men!" No wonder the psalmist concludes the psalm with a plea that God will search and try his heart, his thoughts, and lead him in the way everlasting.

It is hard to know oneself because to do so is to confront the possibilities of human cruelty, pride, seduction, and varieties of destructive passion that are accorded the status of news in the public media. Such human realities are not news. They are commonplace, they are the underside of our own human consciousness. We turn to the papers daily to read about ourselves in the guise of Lebanese bombers, Los Angeles freeway gunslingers, and sexual predators. We pay to be entertained by the brutalities of Rambo, the reminiscences of Vietnam. We watch, horrified and fascinated, as people like us rend and sear human flesh. That is not news, folks, that is the human story.

"Know thyself," the oracle said. "The unexamined life is not worth living," says our Greek heritage.

Ah, but the examined life is not without its problems as well!

Still, to the crowd ready to stone the adulteress, Jesus said, "Let whoever among you is without sin throw the first stone." No stones were thrown that day. He taught that adultery begins in the impulse of lust, that murder begins in the meditations of the human heart.

You see, to know oneself, and to know that we are known, is in some sense to be disarmed. When we are disarmed, we cannot play the old games anymore. We cannot with naive abandon project our destructive selves onto those with whom we share our world.

"Know thyself," said the oracle. "Such knowledge is too wonderful for me," said the psalmist.

"Know thyself," said the oracle. "Lord, thou dost know me," said the psalmist. "Know my heart. Try my thoughts. See if there be any hurtful way in me, and lead me in the way everlasting."

To know ourselves in the inner reaches of our hearts, and to know that we are known, changes us, and can change the way we relate to those around us.

This is higher education for a college of the church that cares about what that means, that seeks to know itself as a community of selves who know that we are known, and that articulates that knowledge in word, in song, in dance, in thought, in deed. A community that knows itself, finally, as responsible to the mysterious God who knows us in our inner recesses and who links us in responsive interdependence to all peoples.

Development of these few ideas about the self in community will be found in H. Richard Niebuhr's *The Responsible Self*, Harper and Row, 1963.

The idea that knowledge of the self in its historical, cultural particularity is the proper mission of the college is developed in John Seeley's essay "The University as Slaughterhouse," in *The Great Ideas Today, 1969*. Chicago: Encyclopedia Britannica, 1969.

Royalties Statement

The royalties that may come to me from the sale of this book will support the work of the nonprofit organization Orphans, Elderly, and Disabled Development Organization, or OEDDO. The organization is located in Kampot Province in Cambodia and provides services to orphaned children, elders, and unhoused families. Medical services and educational programs are provided, including scholarships for college and trade school. Its newly opened hospital is staffed by its own medical school graduates, providing services to poor families in surrounding villages. The organization also grows rice to share with poor families in the area.

OEDDO is one of the missions supported by the First United Methodist Church of Eugene, Oregon. Its support for these refugees of war and poverty is helping these people to have the time of their lives, many of whom have become Christians.

Thank you for your interest and support.

—J. Wesley Brown